3/23

BASIC SPIRITUAL MEANS

PHILIP E. DION, C.M.

D1134928

NEW YORK CITY

JOSEPH F. WAGNER, INC.

LONDON: B. HERDER

Imprimi potest:
DANIEL M. LEARY, C.M.V.
Provincial Superior

Nihil Obstat:
JAMES F. RIGNEY, S.T.D.
Censor Librorum

Imprimatur:
✠ FRANCIS CARDINAL SPELLMAN
Archbishop of New York

(The *nihil obstat* and *imprimatur* are official declarations that a book or pamphlet is free of doctrinal or moral error. No implication is contained therein that those who have granted the *nihil obstat* and *imprimatur* agree with the contents, opinions, or statements expressed.)

COPYRIGHT, 1959, BY JOSEPH F. WAGNER, INC., NEW YORK, N.Y.
PRINTED IN THE UNITED STATES OF AMERICA

Dedicated to my mother,
Sister Vincent dePaul Dion, R.G.S.
at whose maternal insistence
this book was written in filial obedience

Contents

	PREFACE	7
I	MOTIVATION	11
II	TALKING TO GOD IN MENTAL PRAYER	21
III	MENTAL PRAYER—HOW TO MAKE IT	37
IV	THE PREDOMINANT FAULT	60
V	THE PARTICULAR EXAMEN	75
VI	OBEDIENCE—WHAT IT IS	92
VII	WHY BE OBEDIENT?	128
VIII	HOW TO BE OBEDIENT	140
IX	ABANDONMENT AND OUR SANCTIFICATION	154
X	ABANDONMENT AND OUR PRESENT STATE	175
XI	WEEKLY CONFESSION	187
XII	PURITY OF INTENTION	210
XIII	HUMILITY	227
XIV	THE BLESSED VIRGIN AND OUR SPIRITUAL EXERCISES	242

Preface

A previous work, Keys to the Third Floor, treated of the objectives of holiness and positive Christian living. It presented a summary picture of religious life in action and aimed to make clear and practical the distinction between the means and the goal of holiness, and, at the same time, to show their relationship. The present volume, a logical sequel, deals more minutely with selected fundamental means for living a functionally supernatural, Christian life and achieving perfection.

It is not a collection of conferences or ferverinos urging the practice of isolated Christian virtues. Rather, it is primarily didactic in form, and is intended to teach profound truths in a popular, practical, easily understandable way. While its primary objective is not to be a textbook, it could conceivably serve very well in that capacity in novitiates or juniorates where young Religious are to be instructed in the basic concepts treated.

It is intended to instruct the reader, first of all, in the precise nature of certain basic spiritual means of sanctification. Unless one knows the nature of these means accurately, he cannot use them intelligently, and, moreover, he runs the risk of using them badly, and consequently being hindered by what is intended to help. Furthermore, unless their nature is understood properly, there is little likelihood of their being used with much enthusiasm or zeal. Experience proves that no small amount of confusion and fuzzy thinking, if not downright ignorance, about the nature of these spiritual means exists among Religious who sincerely wish to lead holy lives, but fail to achieve results because of faulty or deficient understanding of these matters.

In addition to explaining the nature of the various spiritual means, practical methods are offered for using them profitably and intelligently, not only in themselves, but for integrating them into a unified spiritual life, lived purposefully and determinedly. Religious will be assisted thereby to contribute maximum glory to God and consequently to reap maximum peace and happiness from their life of service to God.

Starting with the presumption of the presence of sincere desires to love and serve God on the part of the reader, the absolute necessity of proper motivation is pointed out, if these desires are to remain vital and fructify in action. But motivation, in the final analysis, cannot be imposed from without. It is essentially a do-it-yourself process and must be realized within the faculties of the individual himself. The normal means from which motivation proceeds is meditation on the virtue to be acquired or the vice to be dispelled. Hence, an extensive treatment of mental prayer is given in two chapters, the second of which explains, by means of a sample meditation, a simple method of making mental prayer which is suitable for everyone.

But essential to any progress in the spiritual life is a conscientious, consistent, and systematic struggle against one's predominant passion or fault which keeps one from perfection. In this struggle, one of the most important weapons, according to masters of the spiritual life and founders of religious communities, is the particular examen. Hence, a chapter on the method for discovering and isolating one's predominant fault is followed by a chapter discussing the nature of and method for carrying out the particular examen as a means to combat the predominant fault and to grow in holiness.

But holiness and positive Christian living are synonymous with union of will with God's will. This union can be epitomized by saying it consists in doing what God wants, and wanting what God does. Such functional holiness was demonstrated most perfectly by our Divine Saviour on earth in His practice of the three great virtues which characterized His life, namely, His obedience, charity, and abandonment. He did what God wanted by obedience and charity; He wanted what God did by the practice of the virtue of abandonment.

Perfection for all Christians can likewise be summed up in the practice of the same three virtues. As a corollary, all lack of perfection and every predominant failing can be viewed as a lack of or violation of one of these three virtues. Because of their transcendent character, the need to understand them well becomes all the more imperative.

Thus because obedience is the very cornerstone of religious life, three chapters are devoted to it: one to its nature; one to reasons for practicing it; and a final chapter to giving practical means for developing the spirit of obedience and overcoming difficulties commonly experienced in living it.

For the nature of and means for practicing the virtue of charity, the reader is referred to the very detailed treatment of this subject in the above mentioned KEYS TO THE THIRD FLOOR, specifically in the chapters entitled Love of the Poor, and Love of Enemies.

The chapters on the virtue of obedience in the present volume are followed by two chapters on different aspects of the virtue of abandonment, namely, abandonment to the action of God working in us to sanctify us through the contact of creatures with us; and abandonment to God's will in regard to our present state of spiritual advancement. This is the point where many well-intentioned souls part company with God's will and thus fail to unite their will to His, and consequently retard instead of advance their perfection.

Weekly confession is a means of spiritual advancement which is rarely used to full advantage, often because of a lack of knowledge of how it should be integrated into the systematic struggle against one's predominant fault, and used as a positive means of growth. The chapter on weekly confession gives practical means and instructions for achieving these ends.

There follows a chapter of practical teaching on the virtue of simplicity as manifested in purity of intention. Its nature is discussed as well as simple tests for discovering precisely how pure one's intentions are in his daily work, and practical suggestions are given for further purifying the intention.

Penultimately, the foundation virtue of the spiritual life is presented, the virtue of humility, of which any misunderstanding leads to regrettable disregard.

Finally, but certainly not least importantly, the place of and the part played by our Blessed Mother Mary in the carrying out of our daily spiritual exercises is put forth, with suggestions for making these exercises more attractive and profitable for the advancement toward perfection.

All that is written in this book is predicated on the obvious fact that the vast majority of Religious are truly sincere in their desire to seek perfection and live a supernatural life. Much abortive effort, of course, is attributable to the weakness of the human will.

But the conviction is inescapable that much more effort is lacking or misdirected because of ignorance than because of weakness, and that many would rise to far greater heights of perfection if they were but aware of the achievability of the heights, and were they but challenged to begin to scale them.

That is the purpose of this book!

"Not to us, O Lord, not to us, but
to Thy name give glory."

CHAPTER I

Motivation

A<small>NNUAL RETREAT</small> is a time for looking back on the year just past. Too often a Sister thus looking beholds only the shambles of the good resolutions she took in retreat last year concerning her predominant fault or some virtue she wanted to acquire. Appalled at her lack of success at another year's end, she says once again to herself or to her director, "Why *don't* I do something about getting that virtue? After all, I want to."

Sometimes, with the help of God, the scene Sister sees in retrospect is not quite so devastated. But neither is it a picture of magnificent triumph or prodigious progress in virtue. At retreat time last year, she hoped this year's retreat would find her quite proficient in the practice of her particular virtue, or considerably more advanced toward victory over her predominant fault or faults. But again this year, such is not the case, as it was not the case last year. Yet, both these Sisters: the complete failure and the doubtfully successful, sincerely believe that they want to have this or that virtue or overcome their predominant fault.

Why this pitiful progress toward perfection which tends to discourage too many good Religious? As they so often ask themselves: "Why *don't* they do something practical about getting that virtue or overcoming that fault?" Dismiss immediately as the cause of this failure the lack of God's grace in a soul seeking to advance in perfection. True, without His grace, there can be no progress. "Without me, you can do nothing." But it is of faith that sufficient grace is always present. Failure to advance, then, should be ascribed to deficiency in *personal efforts* which must cooperate with the motions of grace in all supernatural activity, whether it be overcoming faults or practicing virtue. It need not be said that in all the discussion which follows, there is implied always the presence and action of God's actual grace on the human mind and will in question.

This being so, actually, deficient efforts and scant progress in overcoming our predominant fault or faults are traceable to the ability every one of us has to deceive ourself more completely than another could possibly deceive us. We tell ourselves we want this or that virtue, or that we want to get rid of this or that fault. We think we mean it. But we do not *really* mean it; that is, we do not actually *will* it. If we did, we would be more persistent in seeking and presumably more successful in achieving what we say we want.

True, we admire the virtue speculatively. We think it would be nice to have. But thinking thus, we often subconsciously say to ourselves: "But it is such a lot of trouble to get it. Do I really want it enough to make all that continued effort? After all, one can over-do this seeking for perfection. I will try for a while, but if it gets too difficult, I will drop it." Generally, that is what happens. Or, without going so far as to entertain such cowardly and defeatist thoughts, even sub-consciously, one often concludes that because she admires a virtue speculatively, she therefore has a sincere desire for it. Such notions, says Saint Vincent DePaul, are: "The products of the mind which, having found some facility and sweetness in the *consideration* of virtue flatters itself with the idea that it is actually virtuous." Such speculative admiration or desire for a virtue will not produce the virtue automatically in a soul. Moreover, it will never move the will to adopt means to acquire it by personal effort.

It is only when I conceive a good as practicable and *good for me* that my will is moved to do something about getting that good. Not a speculative judgement, but a *practical* judgement about the goodness of a thing for me, moves my will to action. Holding a tablespoon out to her little son with a stomach-ache a mother says, "Here, take this castor oil. It is good for you." Oh, yes? Little son is not convinced of that thesis. Speculatively, he might admit that it might be good for *some* people, or some people's stomach-aches. But he has not come to a practical judgement that it is good for him. Nor does he intend to. Thus, only by coercion, and not voluntarily, will he take the castor oil, if indeed he does take it. But who will coerce me to overcome my predominant fault? Unless I convince myself by a practical judgement that the unpleasantness of fighting my predominant fault, or the distastefulness of effort involved in acquiring a particular virtue is good for me, is the only course for me, I will *never* tackle the job.

Speculative and Practical Desires Differ

A tremendously consequential difference distinguishes a mere speculative wish to be rid of a fault or to have a virtue, from a *practical judgement* that it is *good for me* to have it, and therefore I am going to *do something about it*. A homely example makes this clear. Picture a young lady, Wavering Wilhomena, ambling idly along the sidewalk of a city shopping street. Suddenly she is attracted by a gorgeous fur coat on a mannequin in a furrier's window. The coat, in itself, is so enchanting that she cannot help being enamored of it. Feasting her covetous eyes on it, she imagines how wonderful it would be to own such a fur coat. She realizes how warm it would keep her on cold days, and how well it would look on her. She can almost feel the admiring glances of friends and passers-by as she pictures herself walking to church enfolded in it on the first cold Sunday of the Fall. "Wouldn't it be heavenly," breathes Wilhomena to herself, "to own that coat."

But all this thinking is merely speculative. It is only wishful thinking. The possibility and desirability of her actually getting that fur coat has not moved her to action. She has not determined to find ways and means to get it. She has not conceived that fur coat as a practical and practicable good *for her*. And so, sighing over the coat as desirable but unattainable, she turns reluctantly from the window and strolls on her listless way. Perhaps she passes that store again and again. Each time she sees it in the furrier's window, the coat arouses all the same old admiration. All her fanciful wishes of how nice it would be to have the coat come back to her. She dreams again of the comfort and prestige and admiration that would be hers if she could own it. But she does not own it. Unfortunately, that is that.

Now imagine fast upon her footsteps another young working woman, Determined Dorothea. The breath-taking fur coat in the window draws her like a magnet too. She stares, admiring it no less ardently than Wavering Wilhomena. All the same enticing visions tumble before her mind. She sees herself in the coat, feels its silkiness and warmth, basks in the admiring glances of on-lookers. But so strong is her attraction for the coat and so much does she admire it, that her intellect flashes down a message to her will (which, being a blind faculty, is unable itself to comprehend the beauty of the coat). The message is urgent. Its substance: "That fur coat is so beautiful and wonderful that I *must* have it!" A dozen objections pop into her mind and one after another are dispatched to her will in on-again-off-again bulletins: "I must have it. But it is so expensive. But it will be good for me to have it. It will keep me warm. But, how will I ever pay for it? Oh, I'll find some way. I just have to etc., etc." At last, all the contradictory messages sift themselves out in her mind. Then clear and unfaltering comes the definitive dispatch to her will: "I've added up everything and weighed all the factors and I conclude that it is good for me to have that fur coat." Her intellect so forceably presents to her will the desirability of having the fur coat that her will, her "doing" faculty, responds with determination, "I *will* get it!"

Once that determination is made, Dorothea takes the next step towards reaching her proposed goal. She casts about for the *means* by which she can execute this determination. Thus she plans: "If I do without dessert at lunchtime, give up movies every Saturday night, curtail my summer vacation, etc., I will have enough cash to meet the weekly payments. Then in several months that darling fur coat will be my very own." The decision is made! She puts her hand on the knob and opens the door to the store and the purchase of her fur coat.

Why did Dorothea determine to *get* the coat while Wilhomena was content to *wish* she had it? The reason: Determined Dorothea made a *practical judgement* that it was *good for her* to have that fur coat. Wavering Wilhomena did not. Speculatively, Wilhomena admired the coat just as much as Dorothea. Maybe she desired it even more because of her greater appreciation of its value. But her wish remained purely speculative. On the flight to reality, it never got off the ground. Staying in the realm of wishful thinking or speculation, it never emerged into *doing*.

The same thing is true of so many of us Religious dealing with a predominant fault or a virtue to be acquired. We *admire* a virtue displayed in the life of one of our companions, or when we hear it extolled in a conference, or read about it in a book. Because we admire it so, see its intrinsic beauty, we think we would like to have it. Then we make the mistake of concluding that because we *think* the virtue is so wonderful and we would *like* to have it, therefore we *do* have it. This, we find from sad experience, is a mistake. Especially do we find it so at the annual retreat examen. We are like Wavering Wilhomena admiring the fur coat in the window. In the speculative order, the realm of *thinking* as opposed to *doing,* we would like to be rid of our predominant fault or we would like to have that particular virtue. But we never get out of the speculative order; we never get over mere thinking about the problem and decide to *do something* about it.

Lack of Motivation

Why don't we do something about it? Why do we let these desires remain merely in the speculative order? Why did Wilhomena not decide to do something about getting the fur coat for herself while Dorothea did? The answer: Lack of sufficient *motivation.* Dorothea motivated herself practically. Wilhomena did not. And without practical motivation the will can not act.

As we know, the will is a blind faculty. It can operate only on information fed to it by the intellect or mind. The intellect, the "knowing" faculty, presents to the will motives or reasons in the form of good for doing or not doing what it does. The will is like a stoker or engineer hidden deep in the bowels of a speeding ship. He is not seen, nor can he see where the ship is sailing. His job is to provide movement to the ship. The intellect, on the other hand, is like the captain on the ship's bridge. He sees where the ship is going and directs its course. He sends down signals to the hidden engineer advising him to make the ship go slow or fast. Similarly, the intellect transmits messages to the blind will, telling it that it is good to do or not to do, to do this or that, to seek or not to seek. This process of the intellect furnishing data to the will about the desirability of acting or not acting is called motivation. In the case of sin, the intellect sends down a false message, telling the will that something bad is good and merits seeking. Like a "seeing-eye" dog betraying its master, the intellect leads the will into satan's trap.

Thus, in practicing virtue or overcoming a predominant fault, much will depend on motivation, that is, upon the message that the intellect dispatches to the will or "doing" faculty. The messages sent to her will by Wavering Wilhomena's intellect did not present the fur coat as good enough or desirable enough to determine her will to say, "I *will* get it!" If the price tag on the fur coat read $29.50 instead of $2950 she would be willing to make *that* much sacrifice to get it. But she would never make the sacrifice involved in the higher price, in spite of her admiration for the coat. We, too, would like to have many virtues if they cost us only slight effort or sacrifice. But $2950! Never!

On the other hand, Determined Dorothea's intellect made the fur coat appear to her will such a desirable, practical, beneficial *good for her* (not for other people in general) that the motivation, in spite of the cost, impelled her will to say, "I will get it!" She had motivated herself to say, as did the Psalmist, "My mind is made up. Now I have begun. Nothing will deter me."

Lack of motivation, then, must be blamed in the first place for scant progress in overcoming a predominant fault, or in acquiring some particular virtue. Progress is negligible because we have not properly motivated ourself. Our intellect has not made the possession of that virtue or the being rid of that fault appear as a sufficiently *practical, personal good* for us. Yet, this is the first and primary step we must take on the road to improvement. Until we are properly motivated to get rid of a fault or acquire a virtue, we can study, or search for, or have pointed out to us all the *means* in the world, but we shall never *begin to do.* Until we have motivated ourself to say: "I *want* this, and with the help of God's grace, *nothing* will keep me from it," no amount of instruction or direction as to means will have any result.

Motivation Is "Do It Yourself" Work

In the final analyses, the responsibility for motivation rests squarely on the shoulders of each individual. Only we ourself can penetrate our own will and motivate it to act. Motives can be pointed out to us, but unless our own intellect assimilates them and presents the goal to our own will as a *desirable good for us,* it will all be "tinkling brass and sounding cymbals." Motivation and determination must come ultimately from within the individual. Until it *does,* until it *is* present, little progress will be made in acquiring virtue or overcoming faults.

Since motivation looms so large in the process of overcoming a predominant fault, we should be clear on how to achieve it. How do we motivate ourself in a practical way, so that our will will spring into action seeking any particular good? Obviously, before the intellect can present cogent motives to the will, it must itself be convinced of the goodness and desirability of the object in question. Such conviction comes only from the operation of the mind on the truth of the matter at hand, since the proper object of the mind is truth.

The intellect, then, must perform its threefold operation of apprehension, judgement, and reasoning on the truth about the particular virtue to be acquired or the vice to be uprooted. To express it more plainly, although perhaps more painfully, we must *meditate!* We must meditate on the nature of and the various motives which would impel us to attack the vice or embrace the virtue. We must mull over, ruminate, and think about all the compelling reasons for and benefits of having the virtue or not having the vice, until the result becomes appealing and beautiful enough to trigger our will into action to get it.

These motives or reasons can be drawn, first of all, from faith, by examining the teaching and example of our Lord on the subject in question; by examining the example of the saints, and perhaps even of one's companions. Reason itself can likewise furnish motives, such as the difficult or absurd or undesirable consequences which would follow taking the opposite course. However, for a practice aimed at overcoming a predominant fault or acquiring a particularly needed virtue, the realm of faith will provide the most fruitful supernatural motives to move the will to action.

No human act is ever performed without a motive. But there is a *hierarchy* of motives. The more powerful the motive, the more energetically one will work to achieve the envisioned goal. But of all the possible motives which can account for one's actions, the most powerful of all is the motive of love. Love is God's own motive. He does all things for love. Therefore, if we are truly serious about overcoming a predominant fault, the most powerful motive we should try to arouse is the love of God. If we will not undertake the battle against a predominant fault or the seeking of a particular virtue for the love of God, then certainly there is no other worthy motive strong enough to sustain us in that persevering struggle. The motive of the love of God can only be aroused by persistent and conscientious *meditation* on the goodness and love which God has first shown toward us. Once we begin to come to the realization of the extent of God's love for us, we can not help wanting to love God in return. It is more practically important to *realize* how much God loves us than to figure out how much we love God. Hence, the importance of *meditating* on and considering God's great love for us. Then, add to meditation unceasing, earnest prayer to beg God for the grace to love Him enough to want to combat our predominant fault.

Since, then, meditation plays such an important part in the process of supernatural self-motivation, we must have clear ideas about it. Hence, it will be advantageous to interpose at this point a treatment of mental prayer before proceeding with the discussion of the combat with our predominant fault.

CHAPTER II

Talking to God in Mental Prayer

THE CURRICULUM of most liberal arts colleges lists a course in music appreciation or, perhaps, a course in art appreciation. The reason is most apparent. Some appreciation of music and appreciation of art is part of the equipment of every truly cultured or educated person. However, such appreciation is very frequently not a natural gift. Some few are born with it but, by and large, the majority are not. Nevertheless, in most people, an appreciation for music or an appreciation for art can be developed. Thus the existence in colleges of such courses as art appreciation, or music appreciation is justified. And what is true of art and music and their appreciation is likewise applicable to the supernatural.

For the most part, we do not naturally have a true appreciation for things of the supernatural. Yet the difference between those who have and those who do not have a real appreciation for the supernatural is the difference between the saints and ourselves. The holier a person is, the greater appreciation does he have of things supernatural and, conversely, the greater appreciation and realization of things supernatural a person has, the more holy he is, because it is that appreciation, that realization which moves him to supernatural action. It is not how much we know, but how *well we realize* what we know of the truths of our faith that influences our living.

Thus, if we are to become any holier, if we were even to become canonizable saints, it will not be because we shall have learned anything new. For all practical purposes, we know now all of the truths taught by the Catholic Church. If we are to grow holier, it will follow only upon greater self-motivation, which, in turn, will come from a greater *realization* of the meaning of the truths of our faith.

Actually, if we have a Catholic high school education, we probably know more now in the way of scientific exposition of the truths of our faith, more of the strictly theological content of the truths taught by Christ, than perhaps the saints did, than Saint Peter did in his day, before there was a development of the science of theology. We know the truths more explicitly, but the saints realized to a much greater degree what they knew than we do. Actually we *know* many things that we *don't realize*. We rattle off the Apostles Creed, but we seldom realize the implications of what we are saying.

This fact of unrealized knowledge can be easily demonstrated. Things known have not hit us with the impact needed to make us truly *realize* what it is that we know. For example, we have heard and read many times in the papers the term "a billion dollars." Now, we know what a billion dollars is. We know it is a thousand million dollars. That, of course, is a lot of money; truly it is a lot of money! But do we realize just how much money it is? Most probably we don't.

But get a picture of it in this way: If we had a *million* dollars in brand new *thousand dollar bills*, mind you, a million dollars in brand new thousand dollar bills, we would have a pile of bills eight inches high. That would be a million dollars in new thousand dollar bills. But, if we had a *billion* dollars in brand new thousand dollar bills, we would have a pile of bills 155 feet higher than the Washington monument! Over 666 feet high! Imagine a pile of thousand dollars bills over 666 feet high and we are seeing one billion dollars. Now when we read that the national budget calls for 174 billion dollars expenditure, we have a faint realization of what that budget is, because we realize what one billion dollars is.

How To Get Convictions

How did we get that realization? We got it by comparing a billion dollars with things that we know. We compared it with an inch and a foot ruler; we compared it with the Washington monument, with the height of a building fifty stories high. We have pictures of those things already in our mind. Then, when we took the thing that was not known so clearly and compared it with what was known, we started to get a realization from our thinking, comparing, recalling, and so on.

Only in that same way shall we begin to get a realization of the truths of our faith which we enumerate so blithely in the Apostles Creed. We know, for example, the fact of death. But do we realize it? Anyone of us standing before a group of people could truthfully say, "I know that you are going to die, and that your sister is going to die, and that you over there are going to die, but I am not going to die." Is not that the way we all think? We picture everybody else dead but ourselves. Did we ever picture ourselves laid out in our coffin and wonder how we are going to look? That is the way to realize death. It is going to come surely! What is the sense of being an ostrich, putting our head in the sand and pretending that it is not. It was such a picture and a realization of death that turned

St. Francis Borgia from a courtier, a gay young blade in Spain, into a saint.

Again, we say that we realize what sin is; at least we say we know that sin, even venial sin, is the greatest evil in the world, the only real evil. Yet, does that knowledge that we have deter us from committing venial sin?

We say we know and believe that Christ is present in the Blessed Sacrament. Christ is there! We say we know that, but do we realize it? It is the same Christ that walked the streets of Galilee and cured the sick and healed the blind and forgave sinners and raised the dead to life, the same Christ that put His hands on the heads of little children and blessed them. He is there in the tabernacle when we go in to meditation, or for a visit, or for Mass. We believe that; but do we realize it? If we did, how account for our attitude? Can we imagine sitting in His physical presence and having our minds wander? Can we imagine our being able to go in and out of a room where *He* was physically present without realizing where we had been or what we had done? Can we imagine our being distracted by something else if we realized who was there? Thus it won't be by learning any new truths about the real presence in the Blessed Sacrament that will turn us into an adorer and lover of Christ in the Blessed Sacrament. It will only be a *realization* of a truth we already know.

What we need in general are real convictions about the supernatural that will regulate all our actions. But the problem is how to get them? In seeking the answer to this question, we might ask ourselves how do we, or how does anyone get convictions in life about anything? How do people get convictions about what they are going to do with their lives, about how they are going to perform some series of actions? How do they get convictions and reach decisions on important affairs in their lives; how decide upon a vocation, whether they are going to marry, whether they are going to marry this person or that; whether they are going to follow this career or another career; whether they are going to be a doctor, or a lawyer, or a nurse, or a teacher, or whatever? How does anybody get convictions about these things?

In a word, they *think about* the problem; they weigh it with all its pros and its cons: "What will be the advantages if I follow this course of action and the disadvantages if I follow the other course of action? If I follow the other course of action what will be the advantages? What will be the disadvantages?" So they weigh both propositions until they find which is the most advantageous and, considering all things, they come to a prudent decision. In other words, they think about the thing, they ponder, they reflect upon it.

Necessity of Meditation

There we have a clue as to the reason we do not have convictions about the supernatural. There we find the reasons why we do not have convictions about the truths of our faith, convictions that really affect our lives. It is because we have not pondered, we have not thought about them. We have not weighed them. As the Holy Spirit tells us, "With desolation is the whole world made desolate because there is no one who considereth in his heart." We have failed to develop a spiritual sanctuary within us. We have not discovered the spiritual powers within us, and by "spiritual" here is meant not the supernatural, but our rational power to think and reflect. We have within us a whole world hidden from all but ourselves. It is the world of spirit in which we share in the likeness of God. It is the realm of thought where we can escape from the prison of our external surroundings and fly out beyond the trammels of our senses to soar freely in the world of

our mind up to the very throne of God. It is a whole kingdom within us where the kingdom of God is and where
we can live as rational beings, delighting in things of spirit.

But so much are we creatures of habit, acting mechani-
cally; so used are we to having our thinking done for us, that
we have neglected to think, and to develop our powers of
thought. Thus, because we neglect to reflect on the truths
of our faith, we so easily fall into natural ways of living,
natural ways of thinking and judging. We judge of things
chiefly by their effects on our material welfare and our
physical well-being. In other words, it is possible to live
practically without thinking; it is possible to live a most
superficial kind of animal existence without ever really
tapping the resources of our spiritual mind, without ever
becoming familiar with the whole thrilling world of spirit
within us.

Because we have not developed our spiritual powers in
stride with our physical powers, we have failed to realize
the privilege that God has bestowed in giving us those very
mental powers and faculties and the ability to exercise
them on infinite truth and goodness and wisdom itself. In
a word, we do not appreciate our ability to think about
God. We don't realize that we haven't even begun to tap
our own mental resources. Consequently, there is often
dislike and sometimes even repugnance for mental prayer,
one of the most fundamental elements of all spiritual life.
So, if we are to preserve our standard of value; if we are
to make advance in the spiritual life, we must retire into
ourself and pursue mental activity with at least the same
effort as we do physical activity. If we are to grow in
the likeness of God, we must, in particular, acquire a
facility with the power of mental prayer which is the greatest kind of intellectual activity possible.

To make certain that their followers would do that, the
founders of all religious communities have prescribed in

their holy rules that a certain time each day be devoted to mental prayer. Generally the rule says that the Religious must devote a certain time each morning and a certain time each afternoon to the exercise of mental prayer, that is, to the exercise of their mind and will—their spiritual faculties. Canon Law reiterates the same obligation.

What Mental Prayer Does

The wisdom of such legislation is apparent. The effect of mental prayer on life is just the same as the effect of food on our body. Being material creatures as we are, at least in part, we do not find in our holy rule a prescription like this: "The religious shall be sure to eat three meals a day; one in the morning, one at noon, and one at night." We don't find that in the holy rule because we are inclined that way and we shall be sure to follow nature in that regard. But because we are not equally inclined to feed our spirit, the holy rule commands that we will take the time to do so. Should we omit to feed our spirit through mental prayer, the same effect appears eventually in our spiritual life as neglecting to eat food would produce in our physical life.

Saint Vincent DePaul, that great man of prayer, says: "A Christian who does not pray is a mere animal in the spiritual life." If a man does not use his spiritual powers, he might as well not have them; and if he did not have them, he would be an animal which lacks rationality, intellection, and volition.

Often spiritual writers tell us that daily mental prayer is like a mirror which we hold up to our souls, as it were. It shows us our spiritual reflection with all of its blemishes just as a material mirror would show us the reflections of our face. But there is this great difference: the material mirror can do nothing but show back to us the hopeless reflection of our face; having shown it, the mirror can do nothing about changing it. On the other hand, the mirror of mental prayer which we hold up to ourselves has the power not only to show us our defects, but it can also point out to us the remedies for the defects. It is through mental prayer, for example, that we motivate ourselves, and come to a practical judgement about the reasons it is good for us to have such and such a virtue, or that we come to a practical judgement about why it is good for us to get rid of such and such a fault.

As was said in the previous chapter, only such a *practical judgement* moves our will. Motivation is not merely a speculative decision that it is good to have such and such a virtue, or that is good not to have such and such a fault. It is a *practical judgement* that it is good *for me* to have this virtue, or it is good *for me* not to have this fault. That practical judgement alone will move us to doing something about acquiring a virtue or getting rid of a fault. And it is through mental prayer, through meditation, that we come to those practical judgements. So, we can understand that mental prayer is not only the mirror in which we see our defects and discover the virtues we lack, but it is also the means whereby we can remedy those defects. By it we can motivate ourselves and determine upon the means to do so.

There are many other analogies that help us to realize the place of mental prayer in our lives. Those who have been or will be teachers will know and hear much about a tool called the "plan book" in which the teacher must write down explicitly for each day precisely what matter she is going to teach, what objective she hopes to achieve in teaching it, and what devices or projects she will employ to teach the matter in order to reach these objectives. Frequently and unannounced, the supervisor drops in to inspect the "plan book" and see that it is up to date. So, our meditation is, as it were, our spiritual "plan book" for the day.

We talk over with God the objectives we hope to accomplish in overcoming vice and acquiring virtue, and the means whereby we are going to do it. It is our preparation for the day's work, preparation for the heat and the burden of the day in the vineyard of the Lord.

To change the figure again, if we observe a commercial garage, where great fleets of trucks are put up for the night, we notice in the morning, before the trucks go out to start the day's work, that men are busily checking the air pressure in the tires; they are putting oil in the crank cases; they are filling the radiators with water and the tanks with gas; they are preparing each truck for the burden and the heat of the day. That is what mental prayer is to us in the morning. It is our spiritual fueling, so to speak, preparing and fitting us to face the burden and the heat and problems of the day in our service of the Lord, and in our work in the Vineyard of the Lord.

Again, our mental prayer is simply the talking over of ourselves with God each day. It is a conversation with God about Him and us. It is called mental prayer to distinguish it from vocal prayer in which we recite formulas and say them with our lips. Mental prayer, on the other hand, stresses the use of the mental faculties, the memory and imagination and particularly the mind and the will. Now, there is nothing wrong with talking to God with our lips informally during the time of mental prayer, but essentially it is an exercise of the higher faculties of the mind and will aided by the imagination and the memory.

Imagination, Memory, Mind in Mental Prayer

First of all we use our imagination and memory. Sometimes the point of meditation is read in common out of a book, or perhaps we read something ourselves. This is the "self-starter" of mental prayer. However, a warning word is imperative here. In no sense must the time of mental prayer be turned into a time of uninterrupted reading from a spiritual book. Such a practice of continuous reading during mental prayer time is a flagrant abuse sometimes indulged by those unwilling to make the continued effort involved in pursuing mental prayer. Not only does this irregularity rob God of the service of prayer we owe Him, but it also deprives the soul of the strength and nourishment it needs, and which can be obtained in no other way than by mental prayer. Further, to say the least, it is not according to the spirit of the Code of Canon Law which prescribes that Religious make daily mental prayer. But mental prayer is a distinct exercise from spiritual reading, or lecture as it is sometimes called.

Now, to return to our topic, from the points of meditation or segment of a book which we have read as a "starter," we recall with our memory various scenes from the life of our Lord, or examples we have seen of the virtue or the vice in action. If we can not recall from memory, then we can invent them with our imagination. For example, if we have read about some scene in the life of our Lord, we can reconstruct it with our imagination, we can picture our Lord there, or our Blessed Mother, or Saint Joseph if it is the childhood of our Lord. Thus, we use the faculties of memory or imagination.

From these pictures or images thus constructed, we then extract with our mind the *ideas* that are contained therein. We begin to think of and consider the ideas that are brought up by these images. For example, in the meditation at hand, what virtue is being demonstrated by this saint or by our Lord? What virtue is he practicing, or what vice is he telling us to avoid? Or, it may be that the meditation topic is God Himself or one of His attributes—His goodness, His mercy, His justice, His holiness, or some other truth of our faith. We think about it. We ask: What is the lesson in this truth for me? What can I learn from it, and so on. Or, we ask, why should I have this virtue or why should I get rid of this vice? Thus, we have used our imagination and our memory and ultimately our minds to think thoughts about God or some particular virtue or vice. But all of this is really only the preparation for true mental prayer.

Acts of the Will in Mental Prayer

We have not begun to pray until we start to use our *will*. The purpose of this reflection with our mind, the purpose of thinking at meditation is not to have the beautiful thoughts, but that the thoughts might move our will to act, that is, might move our will to *make acts*.

But what is meant by acts of the will? Here are some examples: to tell God that we love Him; to tell God that we are sorry for having hurt Him; to tell God we want to make reparation; to tell God how wonderful he is; to tell God we hope in Him or to tell Him we believe in Him, or to tell God that we would like to console Him for all the sins that were committed last night—all these are acts of the will. It is only when we begin to make such acts as these with our will that we begin to get at the heart of prayer, that we really pray.

There is nothing wrong, as has been said, with vocalizing these acts with our lips, telling God in our own words that we love Him. There is nothing wrong with such speaking, but it is not necessary. We can tell Him all that with just a glance of the heart looking up at the tabernacle. We can tell God that we love Him, or that we are sorry, or that we hope in Him, or how wonderful He is, or how much we thank Him, or we can ask Him for something, all without a word passing our lips.

These acts of the will are sometimes called affections in spiritual books. Because they are called affections, many think that they are functions that have to be accompanied by a facsimile of goosepimples, which is not true at all. We don't have to *feel* these affections. They are acts of our will and not of our sensible appetite. Even though we feel cold as ice and dry as ashes, if we kneel in meditation and tell God we love Him, tell Him we're sorry, tell Him we hope in Him, or make any one of these acts as the Holy Spirit moves us to make them—we *are praying!* That is what we achieve by our affections, and that is the goal we hope to reach by reason of the considerations we have previously thought.

When we have thought in our minds of how wonderful God is, of how good He is, how good the saints have been, and so on, we are moved to ask Him to make us good, to tell Him we love Him, to tell Him we are sorry. Our *will* is moved to action by the grace of the Holy Spirit. Just as soon as we feel our will being moved by the Holy Spirit, we should begin to make these acts and continue to make them as long as we can. If we find that we stop after a while, we can go back to thinking a bit more, like a youngster giving his scooter another push with his foot as he slows down. But we must keep in mind that we are aiming to make acts of our will. Remember that! Remember, too, that they can be made wordlessly, with a simple glance of the heart, or, if we prefer, we can pronounce them with our lips. God loves them either way.

Resolutions in Mental Prayer

Finally, at the end of our meditation, if it is to be practical, our will will formulate some kind of resolution. But this resolution need not flow directly from or be "about" the subject read at the meditation. First and foremost it should concern our practice or predominant fault.

It is simple to make a resolution bearing upon our predominant fault flow from meditation on any subject. The notion of a spiritual practice and our predominant fault will be treated more fully in a later chapter. For the present, let it be noted that it refers specifically to some particular virtue we are trying to acquire or some particular vice we are trying to get rid of. Sensibly, we should make the same resolution about that virtue or that vice every day in the week, for weeks or months at a time. We didn't get the bad habit overnight and we are not going to get the opposite good habit overnight. If we wanted to play the piano, we would not practice the piano on Monday, and the drums on Tuesday, and the saxophone Wednesday, and the tuba Thursday, and something else on Friday, and on Saturday get back to the piano again, and then repeat the cycle weekly. No, we would practice the piano *every* day of the week. So, too, if we are trying to acquire humility, or simplicity, or charity, or patience, we practice that virtue in particular every day, and that is what we should take a resolution about every day.

But, how can this be done in conjunction with our daily morning meditation, the subject of which varies each day? Well, in any meditation, if it has become true prayer in our will, we have been making *acts* of love of God; we have been telling God with our will that we love Him. Nearing the end of the meditation, the time comes to take our resolution. No matter what the subject of meditation has been, if it has led us to make acts, we are telling God we love Him. It is the simplest thing then, to say, "And to *prove* that I love You, dear Lord, I resolve that today at such and such a time, in such and such a place, I am going to do so and so about my particular practice." This can be done whether my practice had anything to do with the topic of meditation or not. The proof of the love we say we have for God is what we do to show our love.

In this way we can make a resolution about our practice

flow from any meditation. For example, again, suppose we are making acts of reparation to God. At resolution time we can say: "And to show You that I want to make reparation, I resolve today that at such and such a time, in such and such a place, when I am tempted to do so and so, I am going to do thus and so as an act of reparation."

Again, suppose we were making acts of sorrow: "To show You that I am sorry for having offended You in the past, I am going to do such and such today." That is, I renew my resolution about my particular practice. But it is substantially the *same* resolution each day.

Now, of course, there is no law against taking some little resolution that flows directly from the topic of our meditation, some little isolated act or acts that we are going to do that day. But while there is nothing to prevent this, we must not lose sight of our main objective in these daily resolutions. Our main objective is to overcome our predominant fault. If we had a boat in the river, there would be little sense spending our time on holidays polishing the brass rails and the lanterns, to make it look nice, if there were a hole in the bottom of the boat. Sometimes in the spiritual order we can spend time striving for "decorative" virtues that we would like to have or that would make us "look" good, while we neglect the disastrous hole in the bottom of the boat, our predominant fault.* So, other resolutions may be auxiliary, but we must remember that we can not hope to accomplish anything with scatter shots —taking a resolution today about charity, tomorrow humility, the next day simplicity, and the next day neatness, and the next day prudence. When we do that, we are practicing everything and learning nothing. So, our daily resolution

---

* Just as it is not so pleasant or glamorous to work in the oily bilge fixing the bottom of a boat, so it is not so pleasant concentrating on those fundamental faults and vices we have as is striving to practice some of the more glamorous virtues we fancy ourselves possessing. But it is essential to work on those faults.

should be about our particular practice or predominant fault, and it can flow very easily from any topic of meditation.

Further, it is a good thing, particularly in the beginning of our spiritual life, to write down our resolution that we take at meditation. We don't have to write it down in the chapel, but after breakfast we can write it in a little book or on a scrap of paper. When we have written it down, we have challenged ourselves psychologically, and when the time comes to keep the resolution, we have that added power of recall because of the added sense perception involved in writing and seeing our resolution written. At the end of the day, we can tear up what we have written or save it in a little book for later reference. It is our own private little possession, but the fact that we have written it gives us an added little recall factor and stimulus when we are tempted not to keep it throughout the day.

All this, then, in broad, bold strokes is what mental prayer is. It is the using of our mental faculties, our imagination and memory, to aid us to have ideas with our minds, to have thoughts about the subject proposed, or about God, or about some attribute of God, or some virtue in the life of our Lord or the saints. And the purpose of thinking the thoughts is to move our will to make acts—acts of love, of faith, hope, contrition, sorrow, adoration, acts made in our own words, whether expressed or not.

It is important to note that these acts need not at all be felt; they only have to be made, and to be *meant* with our will. That is the important thing. The less we feel like making them, the more valuable they are in the eyes of God, if we force ourselves to make them. This is so because then we are praying, not for the satisfaction we are receiving, but simply because God wants us to be praying to Him and we *are* praying to Him with our will, not to please us but to please Him. When it is the greatest struggle, our prayer is most valuable! Always remember that only one failure is possible in spiritual life, and that is to stop trying.

In this chapter, we have been discussing in particular the *what* and the *why* of the process of talking with God which is called mental prayer. We now move on to treat in greater detail the *means* of mental prayer, or *how to* talk with God.

CHAPTER III

Mental Prayer—How To Do It

THE VERY FIRST STEP, one that would hardly seem to need pointing out as a means for mental prayer, is the necessity for preparation. "Before you pray," says the Holy Spirit, "prepare thy soul and be not as the man who tempts God."

Suppose we, as a novice, were about to go to the director or mistress to ask some momentous favor. Suppose we are going to ask whether we could go home for the week-end! No doubt we would pace up and down the corridor outside the office for a considerable time, thinking how we could best present our case, the best reasons we could offer as to why this favor should be granted, and the strongest motives to move him or her to grant it. In other words, we would not suddenly get an inspiration that we wanted to go home for the week-end and dash right in and blurt out our request for permission. Rather, we would plan very carefully how we would present our case.

The same planning and preparation is necessary for success in mental prayer. We should think beforehand of to whom it is we are about to speak; of what a tremendous privilege it is that God permits us to speak to Him in prayer at any time we want. If He allowed us to pray to Him only once a week or once a month, it would be an invaluable favor. But instead, He permits us to pray to Him at any time we want. For that reason, and because what we have to pray for is so important, our prayer is deserving of very careful preparation. Now, preparation for mental prayer is customarily divided into remote and proximate preparation.

Remote Preparation for Mental Prayer

Remote preparation for prayer consists, among other things, in our having habitually the proper dispositions conducive to prayer.

One of these, and perhaps the most important, is the disposition of humility. We must have some degree of humility if we are going to have any success in mental prayer or in exercising the functions of our soul in a prayerful way. We have to have sufficient humility not to brood over real or imagined injuries or slights.

Furthermore, we must have sufficient humility not only not to brood over them but also to be willing to *forgive* them. We have to make up our mind that if we are going to nurse within our heart antipathies, dislikes, imagined or real injuries, we are never going to have much success in mental prayer, because those very things and not the thought of God will come into our mind everytime we have a quiet moment. The devil will see to it.

So often we rehearse all the slights and slurs that were said or done to us; we recall what we should have said, and resolve what we will do and say the next time it happens. Such an attitude suffocates the flame of love of God in meditation. Unless we have sufficient humility to be willing to forgive and to forget injuries and to try to overcome antipathies and dislikes, we shall never have much success in mental prayer. Therefore, the first part of the remote preparation for mental prayer will consist in trying to acquire some degree of humility.

The next fundamental disposition that could be considered part of remote preparation for mental prayer is an habitual fidelity to the will of God, especially as His will is manifested to us in our holy rule. The rule is God's will for us. We know that with the certainty of faith. Thus, if we ever hope to attain any intimacy with God in prayer, which necessarily involves our telling Him that we love Him, since prayer is a relationship of love with God, there can not be any habitual, deliberate violations of His will as manifested in our holy rule. If there is, then, the very first time we try to tell God in prayer that we love Him, there will rise like a specter between us the picture of the rule we habitually break and have no intention of keeping. We try to tell Him we love Him and He keeps saying: "If you love me, how about this rule you continually break? If you love me, you wouldn't do so and so. If you love me, keep my commandments."

The rule, let it be repeated, is God's will for us. Whether we are beginners in the spiritual life and community life, or whether many years lie behind us, we must labor to develop a love for and a fidelity to the rule. This is not a question of choice. We entered an agreement with the community when we made application and were accepted. We have ratified a contract with the community to live up to the conditions under which we were accepted, and the conditions under which we were accepted were these: that we voluntarily accepted the rule and would do our best to live by it.

Again, let it be emphasized, this is no longer a matter of choice for us. We cannot decide and have no right to decide which rules we shall keep or which rules we shall not keep. We did not have to come to the community, nor do we have to stay. But if we do stay voluntarily, then God expects us to keep the rule and will call us to account for our observance of each and every rule as long as we are in the community.

This is not to say that each and every rule in our book of rules is commanded under pain of sin, because they are not. However, if a rule which is not commanded otherwise than in the rule is deliberately broken, such an act is rarely without sin, not because of the binding force of the particular rule, but because of the motive for which the rule was broken. For example, if one fails to get to bed on time according to rule, it might not be sinful by reason of the binding force of the rule itself, but the motive for which one does not get to bed on time will rarely be anything else but sensuality, slothfulness, or self-indulgence. Again, if one indulges in reading which is forbidden by the rule, while it might not be sinful by reason of the rule, it will rarely be without some degree of culpability if it is deliberate by reason of negligence or curiosity. The natural law forbids us to act from unreasonable or inordinate motives, and if a motive is inordinate, we do have sin. However, to appeal to a motive of fear of sin instead of love to urge a Religious to obey the rule is highly unworthy of one who has consecrated himself to God. The very fact that we accepted the holy habit is a visible reminder of our moral contract with God and the community.

The community, when it accepted us, took on its own obligations and its own responsibilities in our regard. It assumed the obligation to teach us, to develop us, to show us the way to sanctity, according to its own particular spirit. We, on the other hand, took upon ourselves the obligation and the duty (it is not a question of free choice), the obligation and the duty to be faithful to the prescriptions of the rules and the customs. That obligation embraces not only our external observance of them but likewise our sincere and honest effort to put on their very spirit.

Consequently, if we hope to attain any degree of intimacy with God in mental prayer, such an attitude of mind, such a love for the rule, and devotion to the rule, and fidelity to the rule must be developed from the very beginning.

Remote preparation, then, for mental prayer consists in developing the dispositions proper to prayer, or dispositions of soul which are necessary conditions of prayer; and prominent among these are the dispositions of humility and fidelity to God's will as manifested to us in the holy rule.

Proximate Preparation for Mental Prayer

The *proximate* preparation for mental prayer takes place the night before and immediately preceding the meditation in the morning. We hear, as a rule, the points read for us at our night prayers. From that time until we go to sleep, we prepare proximately for our meditation by mulling over, as it were, the topic of meditation, trying to recall what we know about it, what we've heard about it and read about it. We try to plan what we hope to get out of the meditation. Again, in the morning, from the time we rise, and while on our way to chapel, we recall our thoughts of the night before. Finally, the immediate preparation consists in acts of faith, adoration and thanksgiving, and sorrow and humility which we make to enlist God's help in our prayer. These acts are frequently provided for in the community formulary of morning prayers said in common immediately preceding our meditation. So, preparation for mental prayer consists in disposing ourselves, getting ourselves in condition for prayer both remotely and proximately.

As to the means of making the prayer itself, many of the saints and spiritual writers have devised different and varying *methods* of mental prayer. A method of prayer, quite simply, is a scheme or device or aid to help us direct and apply our faculties to the topic at hand and thereby achieve the objective of mental prayer, namely, union with God in our minds and in our wills.

Of all the methods that have been left to us by all the saints, there is none, perhaps, which is more effective and none which is more simple or logical than the one recommended to us by Saint Vincent DePaul. He makes no claim to have originated this method, but we are grateful that in his words and works passed down to us, he has insisted upon it so much as a means of meditation for his own religious sons and daughters and also as a means of preaching for his sons. It is a method that can be applied to anything that involves the arrangement of ideas; for example, to selling, to giving a talk, to preaching, to writing a composition or essay, to meditating. It gets simply right at the essence of things.

A Method for Mental Prayer

Perhaps the main phases of Saint Vincent DePaul's method of mental prayer can best be demonstrated in action by an example. Suppose the door bell rang one morning and your mother answered it. A salesman stood at the door holding a suitcase and asked if he might come in and take a few minutes of her time. She took him into the front parlor and he opened the suitcase and took out a strange apparatus the like of which she had never seen before. As he deftly assembled it, he began to explain to her its function.

It was, as she discovered, a new kind of vacuum cleaner. He told her and demonstrated to her what the vacuum cleaner would do. "You see, madam, you don't have to dirty your hands to empty the bag, because it has this disposable bag in it; this attachment is for cleaning the draperies; when you need your upholstery cleaned, you don't have to call the man to take the furniture out of the house, because this nozzle fits right down in back of any chair cushion; with this gadget you clean the radiators. Think, madam, of the money you spend to have your rugs cleaned each year. Now, we have a simple rug shampoo device that goes with this machine that will save all that expense. In addition to that, by putting this spray gun to your machine, you can de-moth all your closets." Thus he would go on and tell your mother all about *what* the machine was and *what* it would do—the *nature* of it.

Then, as he could see her admiration of it increasing, he would begin to explain to her *why* she should have it. Think of all the leisure time she would have! Think of all the time she now spends fiddling with that old vacuum cleaner; and furthermore, Mrs. Brown next door just purchased one of these new machines and certainly she wouldn't want Mrs. Brown to have something that she did not have. Perhaps your mother demurs and says, "Well, I like it very much, but I'll have to wait until my husband comes home." The salesman has an answer for that! He asks immediately: "Well, madam, what day does your husband stay home and do the housework? I will gladly come and demonstrate it for him; and I know if he saw how much work it was going to save you, he would want you to have it."

Finally, your mother would say, "Well, it really is a wonderful machine. I would love to have it, and I feel sure John would like me to have it, but I don't know how we are ever going to afford it." *She* doesn't know, but the salesman does! He would be ready at hand to tell her exactly *how* she could acquire it. He would tell her that if she would just put away twenty-five cents a day, give up those weekly movies, and so on, she could easily meet the weekly payments, and make a painless acquisition of this new household marvel.

Now, what has the salesman done? First of all, he told her *what* this beautiful machine is, and what it will do for her. Then he told her *why* she should have it. Finally, and most important of all, he very practically got down to brass tacks and told her exactly *how* she could acquire it and make it her own.

That, in a nutshell, is Saint Vincent DePaul's method of mental prayer. Three little words characterize it: *What* is the thing, *why* should I have it, or get rid of it, and *how* can I do it. *What! Why!* and *How!* The *nature*, the *motives*, and the *means*. If we remember those three little words, what, why, and how, we have three hooks upon which to hang all our thoughts at meditation. We have the framework on which to build our mental prayer, just like the dress form on which dressmakers fashion a gown. *What* is the thing? If it is a virtue, what is the virtue? What is the nature of it? What does it look like in action? Then, *why* should I have it, if it's a virtue? If it's a vice, pride or unkindness or some other fault, why should I get rid of it? Finally, *how* can I do so? What means can I adopt to enable me to do this?

The Method Applied

This method can be applied to any subject of meditation conceivable. Suppose, for example, we are meditating on a scene from the life of our Lord. We proceed in the order listed on a theater program. Such a program gives the scene, cast of characters, and the various acts. Hence, in such a program, we might read: the scene: London 1824. Cast of Characters: then the characters would be listed, and finally the acts of the play.

So, in meditating on a scene or event in the life of our Lord, we first picture the scene. Perhaps it is our Lord going to Bethany, or returning to Jerusalem, or some other scene from His life. What time in his life was it? His youth, public life, after the Resurrection? Then we think of the cast of

characters. Who was there? The apostles, our Lord? Any
enemies of his? Was Lazarus there? Martha and Mary?
Who were the characters? Then we try to recall what they
said. What did they do?

All this takes place in and involves using our imagination
and our memory. Then, if the meditation is to become practical, we ask what is the lesson in this event for us? What
can we learn here from this scene? In any scene from the
life of our Lord, we can learn the lesson of almost any virtue
—humility, meekness, patience, love. Once we have determined what virtue or what lesson our Lord is teaching us
here, we ask ourselves: what is the *nature* of this lesson or
virtue actually? What is it in itself? How is our Lord manifesting it here? Do we know anybody else who manifests it?
Do we observe anyone around us who practices this virtue
well? *What* is the virtue?

Then we ask ourselves, *why* should we have it? What did
our Lord say about it and the necessity of having it? What
do the commandments say about it? Is it part of the duties
of our state in life?

Finally, we ask ourselves how can we get it? First of all, do
we have it at all? Do we fail in it? Where do we fail? Oh,
yes! that is where we fail the most, in that chapter of the
rule about charity. That is the area in which we must do
something about this. Therefore, we will take a resolution
about it. We resolve that today, at such and such a time, in
such and such a place, when we are tempted to do so and
so, we will pray and do the opposite.

That, in brief, is how we use our faculties on our framework of: *what* is the thing? *Why* should I have it, or why
should I get rid of it? And *how* can I achieve this end?

A Sample Meditation

At this point, perhaps a little sample meditation would

help to clarify the process just explained. Therefore, let us suppose the subject of our meditation is the holy rule, or reasons for venerating the holy rules, or love of the holy rules, or some topic in general on the holy rules. What is the first point we are going to think of? The first point is the *nature*, or the *what* of the topic. Then will come the *why*, or the *motives*, and finally, the *how*, or the *means*. They don't, of course, have to be thought of in that precise order. That, however, is the most logical order: What is the thing? Why should I have it? Or do it? And how can I? But there is no reason why we can not think about the motives first. Frequently the very nature of the topic constitutes its motives. For example, suppose we are meditating on loving God. The very nature of God, in that subject, constitutes the motive for loving Him, i.e., His goodness, mercy, love, and so on. But in general, the order will be nature, motives, and means.

Nature of the Holy Rules

So, then, we are about to make mental prayer on the subject of the holy rules. The first point to think about, after our immediate preparation, after we have asked God to help us, is the *what* of the holy rules, the *nature* of our topic. We start to think and we say to ourselves:

"Now, what are the holy rules? I have read them once, or many times, or have heard them read. Certainly, if they are anything, they are a guide for me—a guide to my daily living, my daily life. Is there any moment of my day, from the time that I wake up till the time I go to sleep at night, is there any moment of my day that isn't legislated for and directed by those rules? They tell me what to do minute by minute everyday, every moment of the day—thereby assuring me of doing God's will every single moment of my day. I can't miss! What a means to sanctity that is! The rule not only

tells me what God wills me to do at every moment of the day—not only is it a guide to the actions of my daily life—but it also tells me the spirit in which I should do these things. Isn't that a wonderful thing! Whole sections of the rule are devoted to instructing me in what virtues in particular the spirit of my state consists. The virtues which constitute the particular spirit of our community. What a wonderful thing! It not only tells me what to do, but how to do it, the spirit in which I should do it. So the rule is my guide.

"But, as I think of it, it is more than a guide book to me, more than a tourist's brochure. If I want to go though the Metropolitan Museum of Art, I could, for fifty cents, buy a guide book and it would tell me what was in every room and where each thing was in every room. But if I didn't feel like visiting the room with the mummies in it, I would be free not to go that day. I could decide not to go into the furniture section because today, I just want to see the sculptures and paintings. I don't think I'll bother with the ceramics today. But the rule is not like that. I can not pick and choose among its articles and paragraphs, because it is a sacred law for me. When I entered the community, I made a bargain with God to follow this rule. So now I can't pick and choose among its prescripts as to which I will follow. I must follow them all.

"Furthermore, where did this rule come from? When I think of it, it was written by a saint, or one who may well be a saint someday. What a privilege it is to have such a rule to follow. Certainly it was the will of God inspiring our holy founder as to what to write. And if this rule is an expression of the will of God, written through His inspiration, it must be a pretty wonderful thing.

"God made rules for everything in the world. He made rules for the lilies of the fields, for the birds of the air; and *if He made such wonderful rules for them, what care would He not lavish on the rule for my life, for me, who am so much more valuable than they—He told me that himself. And if God moved our holy founder to write this rule, this book of directions for the sanctification of my soul, I must have some idea of how much God regards that rule and how much He dislikes contempt of it or disregard of it, or thinking of it in a slighting way, or neglecting it.*

"So, for all these reasons, dear God, the rule must be a wonderful thing. Thanks for calling me to live by it. Thanks for exposing me to it, for letting me know that there is such a wonderful thing. I'm going to need Your help if I'm going to be faithful to it. How many times I've slipped already! Of course, You know I didn't think very much of it at the time, because I didn't know all that I'm learning now. When I first heard the rule, my thought was: 'Well, if you can get away with breaking it, it's all right.' But I didn't realize the place it had in Your scheme of things, but I'm sorry for that, dear Lord.

Motives for Keeping the Holy Rules

"I've been thinking about the what of the rule and the very fact that I've been thinking about the what, and have seen that it is so wonderful, that, in itself, is a motive for following it. The fact that it came from You, that it is Your will for me is another motive. Think of how many Religious of our community in the world now are living by this rule, how many over all the years of the existence of this community, how many have lived by it and are now saints in heaven because they followed this rule. For all these years, perhaps centuries, it has been making saints out of people, and it can do that for me, too.

"Besides, dear Lord, what better way do I have for showing my love to You than by doing what You tell me in the

rule? *Having the rule is just as if you stepped down on earth and told me exactly what You wanted me to do at every moment. And I'm sitting here telling You I love You. I love You—trying to tell You that I love You. What better way is there to love You than to tell You that I want to keep the holy rules? I want to love You by keeping the rule perfectly, because it is Your command for me—Your private set of commandments that You have given me. I can become a saint by doing Your will. If sanctity means doing Your will and keeping my will united to Yours, what better way is there to be a saint than by keeping the rules completely?*

"*I remember hearing one time about Pope Clement VIII who said that if anybody showed him a Religious who had kept his rule perfectly all his life, he would canonize him immediately, without even waiting for miracles. That is a wonderful thought for me to have dear Lord. May it help me to keep the rule better.*

"*These rules are Your plan for my sanctity. These rules— I don't have to look around to other communities to learn how to be a saint. Being a saint for me is not the same as being a saint for a Trappist, or a hermit or a member of some other community. Being a saint for me means following these rules that You called me to follow. Their rule is the best for them, and these rules are the best for me. The rules of every community are the best for every community, and only for the ones that You call to those communities. You call all souls to develop differently—to manifest your perfection differently. Even in nature we don't find the cucumber developing and trying to imitate a squash. Nor do we find a squash trying to develop in imitation of a cucumber, even though they might have some similarities. So, You have called each thing to its own particular perfections, and that's how You want me to develop, dear Lord, according to the perfection of and after the manner of our community and not after the manner of other Religious, however praise-*

worthy they might be. But only according to our rules and our customs.

"Now, I want You to help me to do that, dear Lord. You know I cannot do it without You. I need Your help. You know what a failure I've been in the past. I probably will be in the future too but that won't let me get discouraged now, will it? Not if You're helping me and standing by me— and I know You will be. Because, look at how much You have shown me You love me already by bringing me this far."

Means for Keeping the Holy Rules

In such a manner, we coast along in those sentiments as long as we can. Having thought about the *motives* for loving and practicing the rule, then we come to the point of the *means.* Of course, generally when we discuss means, the chief point of approach is an examination of conscience. Where do we fail most seriously in this matter of the holy rules? Is it in the observance of the rules, or is it in its spirit? Which rule is it that we fail in? Is it the rule about obedience? The rule about silence? Or about charity? Our attitude about our neighbor? When we find out which it is, then it is on that point that we take a resolution. Especially we must try to see our predominant fault in its relation to the topic at hand and let our resolution concern that.

But our resolution, if it is to be effective, must be *particular!* We must try to foresee the occasion, that morning, in which we might fail or be tempted to fail, as accurately as we can see it in all its ramifications: the time, the place, the circumstances, the persons involved.

For example, here would be a sample resolution: "This morning while I am in my duty, before school, when I am tempted to be annoyed by so and so, and perhaps show my annoyance, I will *pray* such and such a prayer, and I will say it over and over again until I have conquered the temptation. And I will do this to please You, my dear Lord."

That is a *particular* resolution, with all the elements of good resolution: time, place, circumstances, motive. Then, at noon particular examen time, the keeping of that resolution is what we look for. We don't have to go minutely through every circumstance of the morning, trying to think of all the things we have done and said. We go immediately to our resolution at the morning meditation period. Did we do it or didn't we? If we did, thank God; if we didn't, we tell Him we are sorry and we renew the same resolution for the afternoon, trying to foresee, if we can, the precise occasion when we might fail. The time, the place, the person, and the circumstances may be different from the morning, but the action will be the same, viz. to pray when tempted to commit our predominant fault. At the particular examen at supper we look to that same resolution and then renew it again for the period after supper, picking another time and place in which we are likely to fail. Then, at the general examen at night, we take another quick look at our success for the period after supper. In that way we have divided the day into three distinct periods with three checking points for taking our little daily inventory or trial balance.

Now, it was probably noticeable that even while we were considering in our little meditation the nature of the holy rule, or the motives for loving and following the holy rule, or after we thought about the means, our *will* began spontaneously to speak to God. It was moved to make acts of love, of faith, petition, hope, desire. It is not at all important whether these acts come at the end of the mental prayer, or whether they are interspersed throughout it, or if they come near the beginning. The important thing is that when these acts of our will start, when we begin to tell God we love Him, to ask Him for the help we need from Him, and so on, we should keep on, for that is what is what we are aiming at. The purpose of thinking all the lovely thoughts about the rule is to get our will to act, to get our will to make acts or affections of love, desire, hope, contrition, sorrow, admiration, adoration, and, finally, our resolution. So, as soon as we find we can make them, we should let ourselves go! That is our objective, that is our aim. To make these acts is what we are striving for in mental prayer.

Now, having not so briefly spoken about the means for carrying out mental prayer, it would not be amiss to mention a few difficulties that one might encounter in its practice. First of all, we should make up our mind never to judge the value of or the effects of our mental prayer by our *feelings*. They in themselves have nothing to do with its essence or its goodness or badness.

The Lack of Feeling in Prayer

In prayer, there are two possible experiences we can have as far as our feelings are concerned. When we first begin the practice of mental prayer, God sometimes fills us with the greatest kind of consolation, even sensible consolation. We might think: "Oh, how wonderful this is! I am sorry I wasn't taught all this before. What a wonderful life I have ahead of me. How I love this mental prayer!" But suddenly it may happen that God takes away from us all those sensible consolations, all those wonderful feelings, all that apparent ease and facility. Then we begin to wonder what has happened to us because we are not praying any more. Here is what has happened: We have been judging the value of our prayer by those pleasurable feelings we had. When the feelings were taken away, we thought the substance of prayer had been lost, which is not true at all.

On the other hand, we may experience none of those warming feelings and consolations. Our prayer might be the driest kind of struggle, like being forced to eat a box of saltines without any water. We might get no satisfaction, no consolation from it at all. But consolation is not the measure of the value of our mental prayer, or of the goodness of it. We read of our divine Saviour in the Garden that being in agony, He prayed the more. Certainly He was experiencing no pleasure, no consolation in His prayer. Yet who would dare to say that it was not good prayer? That His prayer was good He proved by His conformity to His Father's will. So too, the effects of our mental prayer and the value of it and the benefit of it are to be judged, not by our feelings, but by our actions, by what we do. For prayer is the uniting of our minds and *will* to God. That is why our Lord said, "Pray always." He didn't advise, "*Say* prayers always," but "pray always." That is, He told us to have our will and mind united to God always.

When we are engaged in mental prayer, when we are struggling to unite our will to God, not because we enjoy it but because we please God thereby, then, we are praying. That is His will for us at that time. Therefore, if, independently of our getting any consolation from it, independently of our likes or dislikes for it, if we go to mental prayer and strive to keep on trying to pray in spite of dryness or distractions, then we *are praying* and our prayer is good.

The value does not depend upon how we feel about it or the satisfaction we get from it. Moreover, the less personal satisfaction we get from our prayer, the more valuable it is likely to be. If we are struggling to pray to please God, and not to please ourselves, if that is why we remain there, then our prayer is all the more valuable because there is no admixture of self-will in it.

The Lack of Beautiful Thoughts in Prayer

Another difficulty must be avoided. We must not fall into

the common temptation of beginners and be disturbed by the lack of beautiful thoughts or what we regard as beautiful or wonderful thoughts. Sometimes we hear people repeat some thoughts that they have had in prayer. Our reaction might be: "Glory be to God, how did she ever think of that? I never thought of anything like that; I don't have any thoughts like that!" Well, we must be convinced that having beautiful thoughts or apropos thoughts is not mental prayer. If God does not give us beautiful thoughts, that is all right. They are not the objective of mental prayer. Beautiful thoughts are, in fact, useless, unless they achieve their purpose, namely, to stir up our wills to make acts of love, and adoration, and thanksgiving, and petition, and sorrow, and faith, and hope, and so on. Thus, let it be clear, the object of mental prayer is not to have lovely thoughts.

Furthermore, for the consolation of beginners, it should be said that the longer we go on in the spiritual life, the more fuel we will have for meditation. As time passes, we shall have had more spiritual reading; we shall have heard more conferences; we shall have studied more about the spiritual life and the nature of the spiritual life. Consequently, we shall have more logs to throw on the blaze in the morning at meditation, fuel with which to stoke the fire of divine love in our heart. Perhaps, at the moment, we are burning twigs and faggots and having a hard job scraping them together. But be not disturbed about that, for, as time goes on, we shall have greater and greater sources of fuel, and the wood pile will grow longer and higher.

Always remember that the stirring up of *acts* of the will is the objective of the thoughts at mental prayer. The thoughts are useless unless they move us to stir up these acts in our will. Saint Vincent DePaul tells us that the considerations, the thoughts at meditation are like the striking of a match on the flint. The purpose of the striking is to cause the spark that lights the match. But, he says, some people are so foolish as to go on striking the match after it has been lit by continuing to think thoughts and strive for considerations after the will has burst into flames of love. If we are moved to tell God we love Him, or that we are sorry, or any of these acts, we must not think that we have to go back to thinking thoughts because now we are at meditation and should be thinking. No. The purpose of the thoughts is to move us to speak with God. Remember, *that* is our objective.

Therefore, let us not think we have to be thinking thoughts if our will is speaking to God. The quicker we can get our will speaking to God in familiar conversation, in our own words—the more personal the better—then, the better also our mental prayer will be. We should strive to talk to God in our own simple, homely, broken English that we use ordinarily. Archbishop Goodier tells us: "I'd rather say, 'Dear God I love you,' over and over again for an hour if I could really mean it, than read the most sublime poem by the greatest poet or mystic or saint, the greatest profession of love ever written." Our own words are better. It is *our* love we are giving to God and we should give it to him in *our own way*.

We know from reading the account of our Lord's prayer in the Garden that he went back and prayed the "self-same prayer," says Saint John, again and again, "Father, if it be possible, let this chalice pass from me; yet not my will but thine be done." We read in the life of Saint Mary of Egypt, the great penitent, who lived for years in the desert, that she could pray no other prayer than to say over and over again, "Dear Lord, Thou hast made me; now please save me; Thou hast made me; now please save me." This was a perfect prayer, an expression of her utter incapacity and inability to do anything herself, and her complete dependence upon God who is all powerful.

Failure to Listen to God in Prayer

Another point in regard to mental prayer that is deserving of mention is this: Because we have stressed talking to God in our own words, with our will, we must not therefore think that we have to do all the talking during mental prayer. It is a conversation with God, not a monologue. We don't have to do all the talking. Some of the time we should listen! Somebody has said that prayer is not like a game of golf, in which one person hits the ball and then walks to catch up with it and hits it again. It is rather like a game of tennis, in which the ball is hit back and forth, from one contestant to the other. So, while making acts of love, of sorrow, of petition, faith, and so on, we should do a little listening.

Again, even when we are not listening, it is not necessary to be talking all of the time of mental prayer. If we have just told our Lord that we love him, we can bask in that sentiment. We don't have to keep repeating I love you, I love you, I love you, like a broken record. We can coast along for a while. We should listen a bit, because God will surely have something to say to us. He is likely to be saying: "If you really love me, you would be doing so and so, or you would not be doing such and such." We must give Him a chance to say what He has to say to us, for in this way we discover His will for us.

So, to sum up what has just been said, our aim in mental prayer is to make acts with our will. But these acts do not have to be incessant. Let us persevere in a sentiment of love when we have expressed it. The same is true of sentiments or acts of sorrow or contrition, or petition or of faith, or of hope. Coast along in the sentiment until, like a youngster on a scooter, we begin to slow down almost to a stop. Then make another act of whatever it is we are making to give ourselves more momentum. When we have given ourselves another push, go along with that until we begin to slow to a stop again, and then repeat the process.

Distractions in Mental Prayer

As far as distractions and mental prayer are concerned, we have to make up our minds that it is not easy to fight them. They are something that human flesh is heir to, and, like the poor, will be with us always. Sometimes they come from fatigue. They come at the afternoon meditation, very often for some; with others, it is at the morning meditation. However, if we are getting to bed on time, if we are getting the rest that the community prescribes, there is nothing culpable in our fatigue or it's relation to our prayer difficulty. In any case, let us face it, meditation is sometimes going to be a battle against fatigue. But if prayer is uniting our wills to God, then the very struggle against fatigue that we make because we are trying to please God, that very struggle to stay awake is, in itself, a prayer. As long as we don't make peace with fatigue, settle ourselves in a comfortable position and give up, we need not worry. That making of peace with fatigue is the ruination of prayer or the spirit of prayer. But the very struggling against fatigue in prayer to please God is prayer itself, because our will is united to His. Why are we struggling against the fatigue? Only in order to please God, and not ourselves, and that is praying!

A further point might still be made about distractions. Unfortunately, we take the same tools with us to mental prayer that we use all day long. The same mind that we use throughout the course of the day is the mind that we use in mental prayer. Thus, if we are accustomed to let our mind flitter like a bee or a butterfly from blossom to blossom, to any thought that happens to come across it throughout the day, without any attempt at recollection or control of our minds, we cannot hope to expect that for half an hour at meditation it is certainly going to be a very tractable instrument, completely at our command. If a mother has brought up a spoiled child who is unmanageable, untractable, selfish, who has her own way at every moment throughout the course of the day, then, when company comes some Sunday evening, the mother cannot expect that spoiled child suddenly to become a docile little model whom the company will admire. It just doesn't happen that way. So, too, with our mind. If it is habitually unstable and uncontrolled throughout the day, if we make no attempt at recollection, no attempt at controlling our thoughts, then we cannot expect much success at controlling that mind during our meditation.

Be that as it may, if we find that we have distractions, there is only one thing to do: come back to our prayer. But perhaps we find from experience that when we do pull ourselves back, we are back for thirty seconds and then we are off again. In that case, there is only one course of action. As soon as we are conscious again that we are away, come back! Involuntary distractions do not hinder the fruits of our prayer, either mental prayer or vocal prayer. As long as they are involuntary, as long as we are doing what we can to avoid them, we need not worry. The problem with distractions is not so much how to avoid them, as how to make them involuntary.

Each time we find we are distracted, we must try gently to come back. If we find that we can't do anything else, let us talk to God about the distractions: "You know, dear Lord, I'd like to be thinking about what I *should* be thinking about. I'd like to be thinking about You. But I just can't seem to keep my mind on it. You know how weak I am. You must help me; this can't go on." In this way, we talk to God about the distractions. We tell Him we want to think of Him, and ask Him to accept the distraction as prayer. Perhaps that is all we'll have to offer Him. We haven't any beautiful thoughts. So we ask Him, please, to take this distraction as our offering for this day. In other words, we try to turn our very distraction into a prayer.

In conclusion, then, the thing to keep in mind about mental prayer is that as long as we are trying, we are praying, and that is the important thing. What leads to discouragement is the thought that we are wasting our time. But there is never a waste of time if we are trying. It is only when we settle back and give up that we waste our time. As long as we are trying, we are bending our wills to God. We are praying whenever we keep tirelessly turning ourselves back from every distraction, when we keep on making the effort in spite of lack of satisfaction.

Again, let it be said, there is only one failure possible throughout the whole spiritual life, and particularly in the sphere of mental prayer, and that is to stop trying.

CHAPTER IV

The Predominant Fault

IT CANNOT BE emphasized too often that love of God, perfection, holiness, sanctity, consists in the union of our will with God's will. It means an active and passive union of our will with the will of Almighty God. That is to say that loving God means that we do all we know He wants us to do, and that we want all that He does to us, or wills to happen to us. The only obstacle to perfection, to holiness, to sanctification, to love of God, to union with God, is the thing called sin, the essence of which is the *lack* of conformity of our will with God's will, or in other words the opposition of our will to God's will. Wherever we have opposition between our will and God's will, whether it be grave opposition or mediocre or slight opposition, to that extent we are imperfect, to that extent we are failing to love God as completely as He wants us to.

From this fact arises the necessity of knowing ourselves, of seeing the deformity between our will and God's will. It is necessary to *know* this deformity in order to correct it. In other words, to be completely pleasing to God, it is necessary to know ourselves and to know wherein we depart from God's will. Hence, the necessity of knowing our sins, our faults, of knowing our failings, and frailties, and above all our habitual tendencies. Shadow boxing never produced a knockout. Neither can we fight an unknown or invisible enemy.

Self Knowledge Hard to Get

But the knowledge of our predominant faults is not the easiest in the world to come by, despite the proximity of its source. In fact, the very nearness of the object makes it more difficult to see. Others we know better than ourself. If we had to write two essays, one describing our own faults, and the other those of our neighbor, we would probably score a higher grade for our analysis of her than of ourself. It is much easier to know a companion's faults than our own. After all, we feel the *effects* of her faults, whereas we don't very often feel the effects of our own. We can diagnose and prescribe for her failings with assurance. Yet the most important knowledge in the world for us or any individual is to "Know thyself."

Actually, we do not really know ourselves until we are ready to say at any moment: "This is my predominant fault; this is the thing that I need most to work on; this is the failing that is standing most in the way of my going the whole way with our Lord; this is the trait that others find most difficult in me; this is the characteristic that makes me hardest to live with; this is the habit that most needs correction; this is the tendency that spawns most of my difficulties." How few there are who can say that on call!

Self Knowledge Must Be Precise

But knowing our predominant fault involves more than being able to give it a name. We must be aware of the particular form it takes, that is, the characteristic way in which it manifests itself. Defective or inaccurate knowledge here explains not only much abortive effort, but also much omitted effort. After lack of motivation, of which we spoke in the first chapter, fuzziness about its manifestations is probably the most common cause of scant progress in fighting a predominant fault, and, consequently, in carrying out the particular examen.

To be practical: suppose we are asked, "What is your predominant fault?" Would we reply vaguely, "I dunno; pride, I guess." Or would we say confidently, "That's easy. Pride!" Before we gloat, learn that *both* those answers, the befuddled and the certain one, reveal no more precise information than did a certain South American amnesiac in the play, *Charlie's Aunt.* Someone asked what part of Brazil she lived in. Her uniformative reply was: "The residential part!" It is equally unrevealing to catalog one's predominant fault simply as pride. Such a skimpy symptom sets a spiritual surgeon an almost hopeless task in planning the proper prescription. Why? Because *every* fault and every sin has its root in pride and is in some way a manifestation of pride, just as every act of virtue is, in some way, a manifestation of charity.

Who can count the ways in which pride can rear its ugly head? For example, one book on the particular examen lists no fewer than two hundred and seven different manifestations of pride as a predominant fault. They range from: "Have I a superior attitude in thinking, or speaking, or acting?" all the way to the opposite end of the gamut: "Do I think, or speak, or act timidly?" Presumably the writer of that list does not pretend to have exhausted all the possible manifestations of pride. No spiritual author would be so proud as to claim that! So, "My predominant fault is pride," is a clumsy phrase that indicates but does not reveal.

The same lack of precision must be avoided in thinking of a particular virtue one might have as a spiritual practice. To be proper, and to be sensible, and to be practical, it must be defined. It must be limited to and pinpointed to a workable, achievable goal. Question: "What is your practice, Sister?" Answer: "The love of God." Nonsense! Surely it is a beautiful thing to love God but it is no object of nor way to state a spiritual practice. It is too vague and all inclusive to be practiced effectively. How, Sister, do you fail to love God? Do you have any faults that militate against your love of God? "Well, Father, I'm a regular termigant to live with. Nobody can get along with me. I'm bickering all the time." Very well then, *that* is your practice, to be charitable in speech to your companions.

Thus the practice must be limited to a definite goal. To say that our practice is charity is much too broad. We say our predominant fault is against charity, but what phase of charity? How does our fault against charity manifest itself? Is it by stubbornness? Or failure to conform to the wishes of the group? Is it against charity in speech? Charity in thought? Criticism? We must pin it down till we know precisely what our predominant fault is.

Only then can we work on it sensibly and systematically. Since our faults crop up in so many diverse forms, small wonder that unenlightened struggling against them is often as frustrating as trying to nail a custard pie to the wall. Hence, we abandon the struggle almost before it begins. A successful campaign against a predominant fault, then, in addition to proper motivation, demands a clear-cut knowledge of the objective, seeing as clearly as possible the nature of our predominant fault and its particular form of manifestation. The more clearly we are able to isolate it, the greater the chances of success in the battle.

Learning a Predominant Fault from God

But how can we learn our faults and our failings or sins? Above all, how can we discover our predominant fault?

Well, there are three sources of knowledge. First of all, we can learn about it by a special illumination from God. Some special actual grace, something we read, something that we hear or see can suddenly make us realize: "My glory, I've been doing that for years and never recognized it, or was never conscious of it." This sudden inspiration is a light from God. If He did not send us special lights in prayer to illumine us as to our carelessness in His service, we would never travel very far along the road to perfection. One shaft of His divine light cast into our souls in prayer will illumine us as to our imperfections more than twenty lifetimes of conscience examining would do, just as one suffering sent by God will reveal more to us about our self-love and will healingly hurt our pride more than a thousand years of our own carefully thought out and self-chosen penances. These split second revelations of God's wisdom flash into our soul only when it is still in the quiet of prayer and not moving about with its own activity and imaginations and human reasoning.

Learning a Predominant Fault from Others

In spite of this, we can never be excused from the personal effort involved in seeking to discover by ourself our predominant fault. Barring God's making it known by a special illumination, two methods are at hand: learn it from others, or search it out ourself. The first way is to learn it from others, a painful process, indeed. So, here tread lightly! Unless we have a sincere desire to be better, self-knowledge acquired from others is only an irritant. Criticism always smarts. We spontaneously resent being accused. Yet, in spite of this, criticism often points most surely to our failings. By nature we judge ourselves more kindly than others do. We don't have to be taught to overlook faults in ourselves which we bitterly condemn in others. We excuse ourselves, accuse others. They do the same.

Further, faults that we often do not even suspect in ourself are so evident to others that they assume we must know them. Thus, they freely speak of them. Hence, if we are sincere, if we are looking for the truth, there is rare opportunity to discover it in the criticism of others. We need only to be willing to shake off the sting and look for it. Too often, we don't. We find a million excuses why this act of ours was really not a fault in us, even though it might appear so to our neighbor. We say to ourself, or to others: "I wouldn't mind if it were true, but this criticism is so wrong. Anything but that!" An observation: the criticism that stings the most is probably the one that touches the rawest wound. Look at it closely!

So, the first source of clues in tracking down a predominant fault is the criticisms, corrections, or admonitions of others, whether they be dealt to us directly and in person, or received "behind the back" so to speak, from meddling or subversive companions. One seriously interested in learning her predominant fault and its more subtle manifestations will examine and analyze diligently the probable justification for any criticism or correction she has received. It may be the missing clue to her predominant fault.

Learning a Predominant Fault by Ourself

Apart from others stunning us with the knowledge of our predominant fault, we have the alternative of digging it out ourself. In spite of the essentially "Do it yourself" character of discovering our predominant fault, we normally get assistance from our confessor or spiritual director. This happens after we have discussed ourselves with him and made known what we regard as our predominant failure, the one that hinders most our going the whole way with our Lord.

When we get our subject of examen assigned in this way, by one who takes God's place in our regard, we have the blessing of obedience on it. We are not doing our own will, but know that we are doing God's will in working on this specific fault. This practice that we need in particular is tailor-made for us.

However, in the specialized circumstances of a novitiate, it is often most satisfactory to receive a particular practice from the novice master or mistress. After all, a confessor knows us only from what we tell him of ourselves, and we are all notoriously self-deceptive and self-prejudiced. On the other hand, the novice master or mistress has observed us and has seen us exteriorly, and knows our reactions, and our inclinations, and so on. Hence, he or she will be able, in discussion with us, by the grace of God and the special grace of duty, to pick out the thing which we need most to work on as a practice, the thing that seems to be standing most obviously in the road of our progress.

Our purpose in striving to isolate this predominant fault is based on the long successful military tactic "divide and conquer." When we are best concentrating our reforming efforts on one particular fault at a time, we gain greater victories than by flailing wildly at too many objectives at once. Such scatter-shooting takes very much trouble to make very little progress. This is noteworthy because a similiar principle serves well in actually segregating a predominant fault. This principle is: "Divide and discover."

To make this clear, imagine a housewife losing the diamond from her ring in a barrel of flour. Furious fumbling in the flour up to her shoulder might never discover the jewel. The whitened tips of her probing fingers might tantalizingly graze the stone a dozen times, and she would never realize it. Her best course is to empty the barrel of flour into small piles and sift them, bit by bit, until she has isolated the missing diamond.

So, too, in seeking a hidden predominant fault. We must try to separate into small categories or divisions all the actions and endurings of our life and the motives which underlie them. We must try to isolate the missing or unknown stone which is our predominant fault from all the other actions and motives and impulses in which it lies hidden, doing its subversive work. We must "Divide to discover."

But suppose that in our search, several faults stare us in the conscience. Any one of them merits a lifetime of work, and all of them seem predominant. We are not able to decide which one is the most predominant, or which needs working on first. What are we to do? What hierarchical order must be observed in the attack?

In this case, the principle of "divide and discover" must be applied still further. In determining the most spiritually profitable fault on which to work, we are abetted by questioning ourself: "What do I confess the most?" A review of weekly confessions for the past year should produce fruitful results. Certainly confession properly integrated into our spiritual life will or should contain a weekly avowal of progress or failure in the struggle against the predominant fault. If we don't tell our predominant fault, what *do* we confess?

Now, among those sins confessed regularly, choose the one, if any, that is most *coldly deliberate*—that we know we commit, yet knowingly resist God's grace given to avoid it, and this, time after time. Again, between two faults, assuming similar frequency, choose first the more grave to work on.

Again, among habitual sins, presuming similar gravity, choose the one *we do more often*, the one for which we have the strongest affection. The reason is that, allowed to continue unimpeded, the habit only digs in more solidly; we acquire a greater affection for the forbidden action. Thus the *Imitation* says: "Resist at first lest the evil gather strength by longer delay."

Pursuing further the process of "divide and discover," additional basic principles will affect the choice we must inevitably make of a predominant fault. Between an external and internal fault, presuming similar gravity, choose the *external* to work on first. The reason is the external fault has the added gravity of scandal or bad example, or perhaps affects the neighbor in an even more direct way, and thus violates charity. "The greatest of these is charity." If there are no outstanding faults against charity, choose the one against obedience, that is the failure against the *active* phase of holiness, namely, doing what God wants. If none, then look for the one against abandonment, the passive part of holiness, namely, wanting what God does.

Finding the Root Fault

A further concept remains to be established as a guide in determining our predominant passion or fault and consequently our spiritual practice and the subject of our particular examen. We must beware of the fallacious practice of treating a rash on the surface while overlooking or failing to remove the cancerous growth within our heart and will which is causing the surface blemish. It is very possible to treat one rash after another without ever really attacking the cause.

In speaking of this subject, Saint Francis DeSales says: "Our examination of conscience must be reduced to a search for our passions. For so far as examination for sins is concerned, that is for the confessions of those who are not trying to advance. What affections are a hindrance to our heart, what passions are in possession of it, in what does it chiefly go astray? For it is by the passions of the soul that one gets to know one's state, by probing them one after the other.* What St. Francis refers to as passion is what we mean by

---

* *Philothea*, part five, chapter seven.

root faults or faults from which other faults flow, a capital sin as it were. What he is telling us in effect is that it is more important to discover what we *are* than what we do.

For example, suppose we think that our predominant fault is impatience. The impatience may be only the rash on the surface. Why do we become impatient? If we analyze it, it is because things do not go as we want them to. Hence, the real underlying fault or passion in this case is attachment to our own will. That, then, should be uppermost in our mind when we are resolving to combat temptations against patience. It should make us alert to other subtle manifestations of attachment to our own will.

Again, suppose we think our predominant fault is criticism. The criticism very likely is only a rash on the surface. Why are we critical? Of whom? Is it not because we have an antipathy toward the one or the ones we criticize? Hence, the real passion, the real basic fault we should be conscious of as we fight the criticism is hatred or antipathy.

By discovering and attacking our root fault, we are able to combat many of its manifestations at the same time. There are two ways of shutting off a lawn sprinkler. We can fight our way into the sprinkler head and try to plug each tiny spray hole with a tooth pick, and get plenty wet in the process. Or we can walk calmly to the other end of the hose and turn off the tap which is feeding water to all the little holes. So, too, concentrating on multiple outward manifestations of our true predominant fault is plugging little holes on the sprinkler head instead of going straight to the basic vice which is the source of the outward faults.

The Two Phases of Holiness

Up to this point, general means and principles have been pointed out for discovering our predominant fault. It is time to descend to some particularized aids for more sharply focusing our predominant failure within our view. By way of introducing them, let it be repeated, in season and out of season, that all of holiness and perfection and sanctity consists of union of our will with the will of God. But this union with God's will, like a medal, has two sides or aspects, one *active*, the other *passive*. Active union with God's will means doing what God wants. Passive union with God's will means wanting all that God does. Any notion of holiness or perfection which does not consider both its active and its passive aspects is gravely deficient. It is only partial if it does not show both sides of the medal.

Actually the simile of sanctity being two-sided like a medal is more significant than at first glance appears. For example, the active and passive side of sanctity are symbolized most beautifully by the front and back of the Miraculous Medal which Mary revealed to the humble Daughter of Charity, Saint Catherine Labouré. On the front of the medal, a burst of dazzling, luminous rays streaming from Mary's hands illumines the path ahead like a flood light, showing us what God wants us to do—the *active* part of holiness or sanctity. On the back, the sword-pierced, thorn-crowned Immaculate Hearts of Mary and her Son, surmounted by the cross, recall vividly their *wanting* what God does, the patient acceptance of all He sends, which is the *passive* part of holiness.

Studying the two sides of the Miraculous Medal in the light of the two aspects of holiness they signify, provides the two broadest and most obvious categories in which we can seek our predominant fault. Ultimately, any predominant fault will be opposed to one or the other phase of perfection, the active or the passive. Either we will fail *actively* to do what God wants, namely against obedience or charity, shown by preferring our own will to his will; or we will fail *passively* to want what God does, namely, abandonment to His will, shown by rebelling against what He wills for us. In these three virtues, obedience, charity, and abandonment can be conveniently summed up our whole duty to God and our neighbor.

Faults Against Obedience

Thus, we could begin our search for our predominant fault in no better way than by asking ourself whether it transgresses the *active* aspect of loving God, that is, *doing* what he wants; or whether it fails in the *passive* aspect of loving God, that is, wanting what He does. First, mindful of the front of the medal and Mary's rays showing the way, symbolizing the *active* phase of holiness, let us consider some common external manifestations of a fundamental fault of preferring our own will to God's will for us in the specific matter of *obedience*. Is our fault a practical ignoring of the rule; a regarding of it with a kind of contempt, especially in small things; especially in those things that nobody sees us doing, and nobody really knows whether we do or not; those things that are a secret between God and us, and God won't tell? Is that our attitude toward the rule? Is that our attitude toward the customs? Do we realize that such a poor kind of attitude indicates the temperature of our love of God, which can be measured by our attitude toward the rule? This is true especially of the rules and customs that nobody sees us, or, possibly, nobody can see us keep. There is the test of our integrity, our honor; there is the test of our fundamental honesty and integrity with God. Can we look ourself in the mirror and ask, "Am I an honest person with God and myself?"

Other manifestations of preferring our will to God's will could be slothfulness and unpunctuality. Our fault might be slothfulness in rising, slothfulness in our duty, slothfulness in our prayers. It might be unpunctuality, the habit of constantly being late, dragging up the rear, rushing to get in line. It might be delay in stopping at the proper time our duty, or whatever else we might be doing. Saint Vincent DePaul says: "The sound of the bell is the voice of God and we should stop even the formation of a letter," without crossing a "t" because, if, up to that time, our writing was according to the will of God, when the bell has rung, it ceases to be.

Still further surface rashes of the cancer of self-will in the sphere of obedience might appear in the form of criticalness of authority, criticalness of order, criticalness of things that we are asked to do. Do we try to win converts to our way of thinking, undermining the spirit of the community and of the house to which we sought and accepted admission on the conditions that we agreed to do what we were told to do? Are we being, in effect, a fifth columnist, trying to tear down all the work that superiors are trying to do for those who are serious? Are we intruding ourself like a termite into our novitiate or community, spreading discontent, undermining the authority, destroying the spirit of the house, which does no one of our companions any good and does us immeasurable harm?

Faults Against Charity

Let us look now for a moment at some particular manifestations of preferring our own will to God's will for us in the matter of *charity*. Do we find ourself speaking of the faults of others habitually, speaking disparagingly of them? Do we remember that every time we have finished speaking of anybody, we have spread peace or war, love or hate, heaven or hell? Do we think that somebody else is better respected or regarded because of what we have said about them, or less respected and regarded?

Again, are we morose and habitually sad, or too serious, or a gloom spreader, walking around with a face that looks like the back wheels of a hearse, thus continuing to be a poor community person? Are we slovenly in our person, in our dress, in the way we keep our work or our duty, the way we keep our desk and cupboard, all of which are subtle manifestations of lack of consideration and esteem for our neighbor?

Is our characteristic fault a certain stubbornness, wanting our own way, wanting things done the way we want them? Are we rigid, unbending, unwilling to give and take, criticizing mentally or verbally those who do not do things the way we would want them done?

Again, in the realm of charity, do we deliberately entertain aversions? True, we can't help feeling aversions. But we can control and avoid manifesting them. Furthermore, experience proves and faith teaches that if we pray hard enough and want it hard enough, God can bring it about that we don't even feel them anymore.

Faults Against Abandonment

So much for some sample indications of preferring to do our own will in preference to God's will in the sphere of obedience and charity. There remains now to recall the love-wounded hearts on the reverse of the Miraculous Medal, calling to mind the *passive* aspect of holiness, and to explore at least superficially, manifestations of a very prevalent root fault, namely, failure to want what God does, failure to conform our will to what God sends us. We are speaking of faults that come under the heading of rebellion against God's will or the opposite virtue of *abandonment*, of passive conformity to the will of God.

Are we habitually irritable when things happen that we do not want, when we are crossed, and fail to get what we want? Do we show our irritability? Are we always whining and complaining about the way things are and asking why they are not different? Is this because things are not to our liking? Do we manifest a lack of meekness in our temper when things go wrong? Do others know about it from the explosion when we make a mistake?

Again, is our fault over-sensitiveness? Do we regard every little oversight, every little act of thoughtlessness, as some kind of insult or offense to us, and give way to sadness and weeping because we have been slighted and overlooked? There are married homes that are run by water power, the tears of the wife. But do we not find that water power has little to do with the running of a religious life? Therefore, isn't it wiser to give up that experiment and learn immediately that it won't work?

Do we give in to excessive discouragement when our work fails, or when we don't seem to improve? All of these faults are manifestations of our disposition of rebellion against God whose providence extends to everything that happens to us without exception.

All of the potential, predominant tendencies and faults of our character which manifest themselves externally, which we have been discussing, are the type of thing which we should mention in speaking of ourselves with our director, confessor, novice-master or mistress for the purpose of determining our spiritual practice.

CHAPTER V

The Particular Examen

ONCE WE HAVE DISCOVERED, with consultation, our predominant fault, it remains to attack it by making it the matter of our particular examination. Actually, there are two kinds of examination of conscience, one called the general examen, and the other the particular examen.

The general examen is made at night, and covers the entire day that has just passed. It is a backward glance over the whole day, adding up the debits and credits, seeking to discover how we have performed our spiritual exercises, how we have done our work, how we have lived our community life. It is a brief retrospect of our whole day, spiritual, mental, and physical, which is made daily at our night prayers.

The point to remember about the general examen is that its purpose is not merely to *discover* our faults, but to tell God that we are sorry for them, and ask his help to avoid them the following day.

The particular examen, with which we are immediately concerned, takes place twice a day, generally before dinner and before supper. It concentrates, not on all of our actions of the morning or of the afternoon, but upon some particular, specific virtue that we are trying to acquire, or some particular or specific vice or fault that we are trying to overcome. This is known as our spiritual practice, or simply our practice.

Concentrating our efforts and attention on one particular fault or virtue at particular examen has many advantages. First of all, it helps us realize the fault more clearly. We have an opportunity twice a day to reaffirm our determination to overcome this particular fault, and also an opportunity twice a day to renew our petitions to God to give us the help we need to overcome it.

In addition to this, because we have isolated it, our attention can focus more clearly on it and we can estimate our progress the better. We are like a woman buying a set of draperies. She goes into a drapery store and is confused by the mass of colors and patterns as she sees them all hanging together. So, she takes the pair in which she is interested over to the window, where she can see them in the daylight, away from the distraction of all the other colors. She can make a better choice then, she can picture how they are going to look in the situation in which she wants them. She focuses her attention on them better.

The same principle explains the meaningfulness and importance of the particular examen. Twice a day we take the occasion to examine ourself on how we have done with our practice, that is, the particular virtue we are trying to acquire or the vice we are trying to overcome. We consider that virtue or vice in itself, exclusively of other faults that we might have or virtues that we might be seeking.

Difficulties in Particular Examination

Mention of the particular examen reminds us that we do not have to be in community life beyond a short time before we discover that it can be a difficult thing to remain attentive during and carry out well the exercise of particular examen, even though it lasts only about a minute. Admittedly there are many difficulties attached to making our particular examen. Many reasons conspire to produce this hardship.

First of all, the very time of the day at which it is to be made contributes to its difficulty. We just have come in from class or school or some exercise, or some duty. After the burden and heat of the morning or the afternoon, our mind is prone to be cluttered with distractions, not the least of which might be the wondering what we are going to have for dinner or supper which is so imminent.

The only answer to the difficulty of time is to face it squarely and motivate ourselves properly. Nothing worthwhile is ever accomplished without effort. If we see the examen in its proper perspective as a worthwhile, necessary, and desirable goal, we will pray and make the effort to carry it out well in spite of the difficulties and distractions.

But even greater obstacles than distractions can prevent making the particular examen well, if at all. One of these is the failure to take a definite and workable resolution about our practice or predominant fault at morning meditation. Another obstacle is the lack of any method or plan for making the particular examen itself.

Resolutions Should Be Particular

First of all, let it be said that the whole success of a fleeting, particular examen will depend on the kind of resolution we take in the morning at our meditation. The very purpose of the particular examen is to see whether we kept our resolution about our practice. As was emphasized when speaking about the resolution in the chapter on mental prayer, it must be particular if it is to be worth while at all.

For example, it profiteth nothing to say: "Today I resolve to be charitable," or, "Today I resolve to be better," or, "Today I resolve to be patient." We are wasting our breath on such generic resolutions and we might as well save it for something useful. Unless we specify and particularize and challenge ourself with the details of the resolution, we won't succeed in carrying it out.

So, no matter what virtue we are practicing, or what fault we are trying to overcome, we must try to forsee at meditation, if we can, the precise time today we are likely to be tempted in this way. In the case of overcoming a fault, we must, in formulating our resolution, ask ourselves when we are likely to be uncharitable, in what place, and under what circumstances? Or when are we likely to be tempted to entertain this antipathy, or to be impatient, or to be proud, or to be stubborn, or to be anything else? Is it after breakfast? Is it while we are doing our duty? Is it at class? Is it at the spiritual exercises? When is it?

If we are able to pin-point it, then *that* is the time we should resolve about: "At eight o'clock this morning, in our duty, or at ten o'clock in our office or at eleven o'clock in the class, when I am tempted to do such and such, I resolve to . . ." but what do we resolve to do?

Resolutions Should Be Positive

Right here, let us not make the mistake of resolving that: I *won't* be impatient, I *won't* be unkind, I *won't* entertain that jealousy or antipathy, I *won't* be stubborn. In the first place, that is not resolving to *do* something but resolving *not* to do something. And *not* acting is always weaker and less effectual than acting.

In the second place, it smacks of the kind of resolution Saint Peter took in all his pride and impetuousness. "Even though they all deny you, I will not deny you." We know, of course, that before the day was over, Saint Peter had fallen on his face. That was because he trusted in himself and his own strength and efforts. We must not repeat his mistake.

Our resolution should always manifest trust in God and mistrust in ourselves. Our Lord said, "Without me, you can do nothing." He did not say we could do a little bit but He said, "Without me you can do nothing." Therefore, our resolution should always be to *do* something, and the something we should resolve to do is *pray,* to call upon God's help *during* temptation. The most important time to pray is in the *midst* of the temptation, at the height of the attack by the enemy. If we should not call for reinforcements against the enemy at that time, when should we do so?

Therefore, no matter what fault we are trying to overcome, our resolution at morning prayers will always be to *pray* during temptation. Hence, our resolution will run like this: This morning, at eight o'clock, in the community room, when I will be tempted to give so and so a sharp answer, I will pray such and such a prayer. Furthermore, right then and there at meditation time, we should determine precisely *which prayer* or aspiration we will say during temptation that day. Perhaps it will be a prayer we will make up ourselves. Perhaps it will be an invocation selected from a litany. No matter. The important thing is to *select the prayer* and determine to say it when we are tempted to commit our predominant fault.

Resolutions and Fire Drills

But there is yet a step further to go in formulating our resolution, which can be made clear in this manner: All the process of devising our resolution bears a striking analogy to a fire drill. The purpose of a fire drill is to pre-determine, in the calmness of a non-emergency situation, precisely what is to be done when an emergency does break out. The exits are located; an escape path is plotted; the location of the alarm box is noted, and the fire extinguishers are spotted. If we waited until the confusion of a conflagration is rampant before trying to decide what to do or how to escape, disaster would follow.

So, taking a resolution at morning meditation is our daily fire drill. In the calm of a non-emergency situation at prayer, we plan precisely what we will do when the fire of temptation breaks out. It is morally certain to break out, since we are concerned with temptations to our predominant fault. If we wait until the blaze has burst upon us to think of what we should do, disaster will follow, as so many of our charred experiences of the past can testify.

Hence, the necessity of knowing, as precisely as we can, exactly what we should do when the fire of temptation begins to scorch us and singe the hairs on our hands and eyebrows. Hence, too, the importance of determining the precise prayer we will say, that is, the exact fire extinguisher we will use.

All of this brings us to the further step in our resolution formation alluded to above. We resolved to say such and such a prayer when we would be tempted. But how many times will we say that prayer on the occasion of that temptation? Would we say it once or twice and then give in to the temptation? How long would we squirt a fire extinguisher on a fire? Obviously, till the fire was out. So, too, we should resolve to say our selected prayer over and over until the fire of temptation is overcome or under control.

The final step of the resolution is to propose to ourselves a supernatural motive for carrying out our resolution. Why are we going to be on the alert for temptation so that we may pray all during it? To please God, to show our love, or to make reparation. Some such supernatural motive should be proposed to ourself.

Then, if we really *mean* that we are going to do this for the sake of God, and if we are truly serious about it, we will add to our resolution this codicil: "If I fail to do this, I will do or omit such and such a thing as a *penance to myself.*" But if we decide to penance ourself, the thing determined as a penance should be sufficiently difficult to be a deterrent to us at the time of temptation. In other words, we would rather overcome the temptation than do the penance. A suggestion: How about memorizing three verses of Scripture as a penance each time we fail to keep our resolution?

Now, one by one, we have accumulated all the elements of a good resolution, we have tried to foresee the time, the place, the circumstances, the action we will do, and the motive. Putting them all together, we have a resolution like this: This morning, at eight o'clock, at common work, when Sister Paphnutius takes the mop when it is my turn to mop, and I am tempted to tell Sister Paphnutius what I think of her, I will say, "Virgin most prudent, pray for me," and I will say it over and over until I have conquered the temptation. I am going to do this to show my love for you dear Lord." Now, if we take resolutions that are particularized like that, much of the difficulty of particular examen will disappear.

A Method for Particular Examen

Having thus clarified the great difficulty with the particular examen of ineffectual resolutions, we can proceed to the difficulty of a wrong or non-existing *method* of trying to carry out the particular examen. Actually, if we are formulating proper resolutions in the morning, we have but to follow this very simple and effective method for a most successful particular examen.

On the way to chapel, before we get there, we should make a serious effort to recollect ourselves, to think of where we are going. We are going into the very presence of God himself. And why are we going there? We are going there to make our examen. So we ask God quickly for the grace to make the examen well. We can do all this on the way to the chapel, in the corridor, or after we get to the chapel as we genuflect. So, the first thing is to be recollected beforehand and ask God for the grace to make the examen well.

Then, since the purpose of the particular examen is to check on our progress against our particular fault or in our special virtue, in a word, our practice, we don't have to bother tediously going over our whole morning's activities. Instead, we mentally go right to the heart of the matter. What was our resolution this morning? It concerned eight o'clock at common work. Did I say that prayer over and over when I was tempted to be antagonistic? No matter what our resolution might have been, I ask: "Did I say that prayer that I said I was going to say when I was tempted to be impatient, or to think those uncharitable thoughts, or to indulge that antipathy? Did I say the prayer?" If we did, we know it immediately. If we did not, we likewise know it immediately. The particular examen is over as far as that point is concerned. It wasn't so difficult to make after all, was it?

Then, if we find we have kept our resolution, we say: "Thank You dear Lord. I could not have done it without Your help." One the other hand, if we did not keep it, we say: "Dear Lord, I said I was going to do that and I didn't do it. Well, never mind. I'm sorry but, I thank You for the help You gave me which I didn't use. But this afternoon is going to be better!"

Thus we examine ourself to see if we kept our resolution. We thank God if we did, and we thank him if we did not. Then we renew our resolution for the afternoon. Again, we try to forsee the time and place and circumstances this afternoon in which we are likely to be tempted or have an opportunity to commit this fault. Will it be during spiritual exercises? Will it be at recreation? Will it be at meals? Will it be doing the dishes after meals? Will it be in class, or in study time, or when will it be? Each of us knows that. So this afternoon, at such and such a time, when so and so says something, or does something, or when this happens or that happens, and I am tempted to be impatient, to be unkind, to be uncharitable, to entertain this antipathy, or to lose my temper, or whatever my predominant fault is, I will pray such and such a prayer and I will say this prayer over and over again till the temptation has passed.

Then, at the supper particular examen we simply repeat our process of noontime. We recollect ourself, ask God briefly for the grace to make a good examen. Then, we go immediately in mind to the point of our resolution, the time and the place. We thank God if we have kept it; if we haven't, we thank Him for His help anyway, and ask Him for His help in the future.

Then we renew our resolution for the period after supper till retirement time. At the general examen at night, we take a quick look at our achievement of the evening. So, as has been said before, we have divided the day into three distinct segments with three check-in points.

This is a simple, effective method for the particular examen. What are the steps? Recollection, thinking of what we are going to do; asking God briefly for the grace we need; then going mentally immediately right to the time, the place of our particular resolution to see if we have kept it. It takes but an instance to think of that. Then we thank God for the results and ask His pardon for failure, and renew the resolution for the next period of the day. That is all there is to the exercise of the particular examen which some regard so horrendous and difficult.

If we carry out our daily particular examinations in this way, then the success or failure we have had all week rightfully becomes the foremost matter we take to our weekly confession. We report on the progress we have made on overcoming our predominant fault or acquiring the virtue we need the most. Thus, there is a sensible unity to our spiritual life. We are not floundering and flailing about like a baby tossed in a swimming pool, just trying to keep our heads above water. Instead, we are going at it sensibly, reasonably, with a definite plan.

The chief matter of our weekly confession, then, will be the virtue or vice about which we are taking our particular resolution, and the fact of whether we are making progress or sliding backwards. If this be the case, it is not going to take us a month to examine our conscience every week. If we have been making a particular examen in this fashion every day, twice a day, or three times, we can rightfully spend most of our preparation time for confession as it should be spent, on arousing sorrow for our sins, not on trying to find them.

Practicing Interior Virtues

Up to this point in our discussion of a method for particular examen we have been stressing the combat against exterior faults in particular. But it is possible that our major fault be interior. It might be an interior fault of pride, of self-complacency, or lack of recollection, dissipation, if you will. It might be a tendency to discouragement.

The way to tackle an interior fault is to resolve to practice the opposite virtue at the time of temptation. It is essentially a positive approach. For example, suppose we have an interior fault of self-complacency, or love of praise and flattery; we preen like a peacock if we hear somebody talk about us or say we did a good job. We habitually refer all our accomplishments to ourselves.

In such an instance, we should make a resolution like this: Each time this morning that I find myself thinking about myself as something quite wonderful, or hear anybody say anything about me, and I am tempted to be complacent, I will make an act of humility by saying this prayer: "Not to us, oh Lord, not to us, but to Thy name give glory," or, "I refer everything to You; not to me, oh Lord, but to You," and I will say this prayer over and over until the temptation has passed.

Or, suppose we have an internal fault of giving way to discouragement. In that event, we can resolve: everytime this morning I am tempted to feel discouraged, I am going to make an act of trust in God by saying, "Sacred Heart of Jesus, I place my trust in thee," or, "Dear Lord, I trust in thee completely," or, "Lord I do believe, help my unbelief." And I will repeat this prayer over and over till the temptation is passed.

Reminder for the Day

In addition to using actual temptations as occasions for making these acts, we can choose a "reminder for the day" or for the week, a reminder to prompt us to make such acts of virtue. For example, we can resolve that everytime we walk upstairs this morning we are going to make an act of trust in God; or everytime we see this pin in our sleeve, or anytime we do anything else, whatever it might be, or anytime any particular thing happens, we are going to make an act of trust in God.

The number and kinds of reminders we might choose as prompters to make acts of trust in God within us, or of any interior virtue, are limitless. For example: Each time we step on an elevator in the hospital; each time the phone rings; each time someone walks into the office; each time we walk up steps; each time we hear the clock strike; each time we hear a plane go over. A teacher might use as a reminder each time she opens a book in class. She might make a mark on the board, an unobtrusive asterisk, a cross, the initials of an ejaculation. Each time she turned to the board, or saw it from the back of the room, it would remind her to make her act of interior humility, or trust, or recall the presence of God within her, or whatever else her practice might be.

Of course, our reminder is only a reminder *as long as it reminds.* We can get so used to seeing and hearing things in their accustomed place or at their accustomed time that we don't really see or hear them at all. That is, we don't see or hear them until they get out of their accustomed place. For that reason, a very good reminder is to change the position of a statue or crucifix on the desk so that it obtrudes itself on our consciousness. When it does, we are *reminded,* and we make our act of virtue.

It should be noted that the same kind of familiarity here can likewise vitiate the effectiveness of a chosen prayer or aspiration or ejaculation. After we have said an aspiration many times, over a long period of time, it can become mere mechanical repetition. We might as well be saying, "Atomic Energy Commission, watch over us." An aspiration or ejaculation is important because it directs our mind to God for an instant. If it ceases to do this, it has lost its effectiveness. That is why it is helpful to change our aspiration from time to time. That is why, also, it is helpful sometimes to try to make "wordless" aspirations. That is, we should try to turn our mind to God without saying any words or ejaculations. Then we will be practicing real prayer, and *really* praying. Then we shall be reminded that it is possible to say aspirations without praying, that is, without turning our mind to God; but it is not possible to turn our mind to God without turning our mind to God, that is, without praying.

Having changed our reminder or our ejaculatory prayer, it is possible that familiarity will again vitiate its usefulness. In that case, we should not hesitate to change it again. For some this can or must be done daily; for others it might be necessary only weekly or monthly. The reminder is a tool to help us to attack our interior failing by practicing positively the virtue that is opposed to the failing. Consequently, we must strive to keep our tool sharp and in good condition.

In this method of striving to overcome an interior fault, or to acquire an interior virtue, at the time of particular examen we merely check to see whether we did, in fact, use those temptations as occasions for making acts of our particular virtue, or when we did go upstairs or come in contact with any one of our reminders whether we did, in fact, make acts of this virtue. Then, we renew our resolution for the afternoon and the evening as the case may be as explained above.

Before concluding these suggestions for making our daily resolution and particular examen, it will not be amiss to propose a solution to two possible difficulties which might be experienced in the practical order.

Unforseeable Temptations to a Predominant Fault

The first can be stated thus: What do we do if, at resolution time at morning meditation, we are honestly unable to foresee precisely any occasion in which we might probably be tempted to our predominant fault? Suppose, for example, our predominant fault is criticism. Conceivably, as we look ahead to our morning, we cannot anticipate any particular occasion that might arise in which we will be tempted to be critical. However, we do know that only a rare morning passes without our being critical in some way. The same thing could be said if our predominant fault were impatience, or surliness or complaining, or any other.

In such a case, if we cannot forsee all the precise elements of a good resolution which were enumerated, namely, time, place, circumstances, action, and motive, then we can do the next best thing. We can select a definite *time* during which, no matter what we are doing, we will be especially on our guard against that fault. For example, we could resolve: This morning, from eight to nine o'clock, in (wherever I customarily am at that hour), I will be particularly watchful for temptations to criticism, or impatience, or surliness or whatever our practice might be.

If we were conversing with a companion as we walked, and saw ahead of us on the sidewalk a glassy sheet of ice, we would, as we drew near to it, interrupt our conversation somewhat, if not stop it altogether. Perhaps we would even take our companion by the arm as a caution against slipping. In any event, we would become alert and watchful until we had successfully negotiated the icy patch.

Like that dangerous patch of ice, is the definite hour which we set aside at meditation during which to be alert to temptations to our predominant fault. As we approach that hour, we can remind ourselves that this is the zero hour, and, as it begins, say a prayer that we may negotiate it successfully.

Thus, while we have not been able to forsee *all* the circumstances of our temptations, we have been able to plan ahead definitely to some extent. Then, at our particular examens, we have but to check our conduct during the hour of the alert. If we sincerely plan ahead like this for a definite, limited time, we can be sure that God's grace will not be wanting to remind us to pray when we are being tempted at other times than the zero hour.

Why We Forget the Resolution in Temptation

The second practical difficulty sometimes experienced in carrying out our resolution is this: We are faithful in resolving, but during the day, when the temptation comes, we commit the fault before we think of the resolution, the very means we chose to overcome the temptation.

The reason is that we have not developed a sensitivity to the beginnings of temptation. We have not learned to recognize spontaneously and instinctively the first signs of approaching danger and threat of disaster. If the average motorist was accustomed to say, as we do about our faults, "I am always involved in the accident before I recognize the danger and think of using the means to avoid it," what a carnage would besmear our highways! The motorist has developed such a habit of recognizing incipient danger that he spontaneously and instinctively reacts to it. He does not have to go through all the steps of saying to himself: There is a car pulling out of that side street at the right. I must now release the accelerator, step on the clutch with my left food, and apply the brake with my right foot. He does all that instinctively and spontaneously, almost without thinking, because he has developed that habit.

Why has the motorist developed that habit in the material order, while we have not developed it in the spiritual order? "The children of this world are wiser in their generation than the children of light." The reason for the difference between the driver and ourselves was stated in the first chapter of this book. The motorist has *motivated* himself to achieve a goal; we have not.

The autoist made the civic right to drive his own car such a practical and desirable good to himself that he loved it and determined to get it. Therefore, no effort was too great a price to pay to reach that goal. He laboriously learned to drive; he practiced stopping and starting, turning and backing and parallel parking. All this he had to do in order to pass the test to get his permit to drive.

But beyond this, for other very strong motives, he wants to remain a good driver and maintain his habit of recognizing danger immediately, long before he is involved in it. He loves his life and does not want it snuffed out. He loves his shining new car and doesn't want it marred or destroyed. He loves his pocketbook and doesn't want to deplete it paying damages to other motorists with whom he might collide. So, lest what he loves suffer harm, he has carefully developed and preserves an alert watchfulness for the first signs of approaching danger, and immediately uses the means to avoid it.

Now, this is a hard saying, yet it seems that the motorist loves his car and his money more then we love God. But, what other conclusion remains? It will be so until we motivate ourselves to love God who has first loved us; until we motivate ourselves to love Him so much and to fear so much to hurt Him in the least way, that we will spare no effort to develop a *habit* of *recognizing instinctively* the first beginnings of temptation to hurt Him; that we will go to any lengths to develop a *habit* of *using immediately* the means to avoid this, namely, fulfilling our resolution to pray when we are tempted.

Until that time, we shall continue to find ourselves staggering away from the shambles of one wrecked resolution after another. Until we have motivated ourselves really to *love* God, to do what He wants, instead of what we want; to want what He does, instead of what we want done, we will be still lamenting the fault before we think about our resolution.

Examen Should Be Forward-Looking

But if that were the case with us at examen time this noon or at examen time yesterday, let us remember that the particular examen must not look only to the past. It is not a question of crying over split milk; it is a determination, first and foremost, not to spill the milk again! The examen should be forward-looking. We don't go to examen to weep tears for the faults we committed so much as to form a resolution not to commit the faults in the future. We trust we are sorry for sins we have committed, but the chief purpose of the examen is to resolve not to commit them this afternoon, or tonight, or tomorrow morning. Let us approach it, then, with a positive attitude. Let us approach it with a new determination to motivate ourselves never to want to hurt God again. And let our motive in this always be the motive of any Christian, not to *feel* good, but to *be* good. Let it be to do God's will.

CHAPTER VI

Obedience—What It Is

MAN IS A SOCIAL ANIMAL both in the natural order and supernatural order. Saying he is a social animal is to affirm that he naturally lives in society. Man is a social animal in the natural order, depending on the familial society and the civil society of the state. He depends upon these societies for temporal goods, for protection, for things, in a word, which he cannot do or procure for himself. In the supernatural order also, man is a member of the society of the Church which does for him the things he cannot do for himself in relation to his eternal salvation. It gives him supernatural help and protection. Those who belong to a religious community are members of another society which corresponds in the supernatural order to that of the family in the natural order.

It is imperative, then, to understand the nature of a society, if we are to live religious life intelligently. A society is a group of individuals united together and working toward a common end. One of the essential notes of a society is that there be a common end or objective. Mere numbers of persons do not constitute a society. There are more people by far on one subway train that runs every two minutes in the New York rush hour than there are in any province of religious in the country, but they do not constitute a society because they are not working for a common end by using common means.

But there can not be a society unless there is authority. Authority directs and orders and regulates the members of a society toward the common end. That is the very meaning of authority—a moral power of guiding the actions of the members of a society toward the end of that society.

No Authority without Obedience

Further, just as no society can exist without authority, so too, no society can exist without submission of the members of the society to the authority. The members achieve the end of the society in proportion to their willingness to follow and submit to the guidance and instruction and orders of the authority in the society.

Now, the following or submitting on the part of the members to the guidance and instruction and orders of the authority in any society is what is called obedience. The necessity of submission of will or obedience to the authority in any society applies to all societies whether it be the Married Women's Society, the Holy Name Society, the United States of America, or the Holy Roman Catholic Church.

As does every society, each religious community has its own proper end. Whatever differing secondary ends they may have, the primary end of them all is the glory of God and the perfection of the individual members. That is the purpose for which those members are united together. In other words, their primary end is supernatural. But, since a supernatural end can be achieved only by supernatural means, there must be supernatural submission on the part of the members to those in authority. That is to say, supernatural obedience on the part of the members to authority is indispensable to religious life. Hence, the importance of the answer to the question: What is the supernatural virtue of obedience?

In determining the answer to this question, it must be said, first of all, that any obedience involves essentially a submission of the will, which means doing the thing that has been commanded. If we are told to go upstairs, we have submitted our will when we have gone upstairs. But there is more to the *virtue* of obedience than mere submission of the will. In order, then, that we may understand the supernatural virtue of obedience more clearly, let us see, first of all, what it is not.

Virtue of Obedience Requires Motive

As has just been said, mere submitting of our will to the will of another is not necessarily the virtue of obedience at all. For example, a convict goes into the prison yard when a guard tells him to go out, and returns when the guard orders him to come in; but such conformity is not necessarily the virtue of obedience. The prisoner *must* submit or risk being hit on the head with a rifle butt. Again, a slave carrying out the orders of his master merely because he fears punishment is not necessarily performing an act of the virtue of the obedience at all, although he is submitting his will to the will of another. But mere slavery is not the virtue of obedience.

To practice the virtue of obedience it is necessary to do more than merely submit the will. The something more is to have a special *motive*. We must have a particular motive for which we submit our wills in order to practice the virtue of obedience. According to the teaching of Saint Thomas Aquinas, the special virtue of obedience is that virtue by which we do what we are commanded precisely *because we have been commanded to do so.**

Obedience in General

Saint Thomas makes an important distinction between what he calls obedience in general and the special virtue of obedience which is proper to the living of the religious life. He speaks of obedience in general, and teaches that it is not a virtue at all but merely a *circumstance* that accompanies any good action which conforms to law in some way. For example, if we did not walk on the grass this morning, we were obedient in the general sense, to the sign saying keep off the grass. We obeyed the law by not walking on the grass; but we did not practice the special virtue of obedience.

Again, for example, our Divine Lord said, "Love your enemies, do good to those who hate you, and pray for those who persecute and calumniate you." Suppose, then, we love our neighbor as best we can; are we being obedient? Saint Thomas would say it all depends upon our motive. If we are loving our neighbor for the sake of God, we are practicing the virtue of charity, the motive of which is love, and which is a different virtue from obedience. But, in fulfilling the law of charity, we are being obedient in the general sense because we are keeping the law. However, if, in addition to our motive of love, we are loving our neighbor specifically and precisely because God commanded us to do so, then we are also practicing the special virtue of obedience.

Here we see the essential distinction that Saint Thomas makes between obedience in general, which is merely a circumstance accompanying any act that is in accord with law, and the special virtue of obedience by which we do

---

* *Summa Theologica*, 2-2, Q. 104, Art. 2, ad 1.

something commanded precisely because it is commanded. The thing which specifies the virtue of obedience is the motive. If we are commanded to do something and do it *because we are commanded,* then we are practicing the special virtue of obedience. If we have been commanded to do something, and do it merely because otherwise we shall be punished, we are not practicing the special virtue of obedience, even though we submitted our will and have been obedient in the general sense.

Therefore, there is a *circumstance* of obedience attached to doing anything that we are told, anything that falls under the law in any way. Consequently, it is clear that every act of submission to a superior is not necessarily an act of the virtue of obedience. To perform an act of the special virtue of obedience, we must have the *intention* or *motive* of doing the thing *because it is commanded.*

In summary, then, for formal obedience, two things are necessary: First, a command from a lawful superior. Second, a particular intention or motive on our part. What is the motive? It must be to do the thing because we have been commanded. We submit our will to the command of a superior precisely because he has commanded us. Only in such instances do we perform acts of the special virtue of obedience.

The Nature of Formal Disobedience

Of course, the opposite proposition is likewise true. If, in order to have formal obedience we must carry out a command precisely because we have been commanded, so, too, to commit formal disobedience we must refuse to do a thing precisely for this motive: That we have been told to do it.* There must be a certain contempt for the command. When

---

* *Summa Theologica,* 2-2, Q. 105, Art. 1, ad 1.

we say we have been disobedient to the rule, most likely we have not committed formal disobedience to the rule at all. Formal disobedience demands that element of contempt by which we disobey precisely because we have been commanded. For that reason contemptuous disobedience of the rule is always mortally sinful, according to St. Thomas.

Therefore, when we speak of being disobedient, generally we do not indicate formal disobedience at all. Most frequently we refer to the circumstance of disobedience which accompanies our failure to fulfill some commandment. In such instances, we should try to discover the motive for which we fail to fulfill the law. The disobedience of which we accuse ourselves is not formal disobedience but merely material disobedience.

How were we disobedient? Perhaps we talked during a time of silence. But were we really disobedient? We were not formally disobedient unless we said to ourself: "The rule says to keep silence now, but I don't care for the rule. It makes me tired. I'm going to break it and talk anyway." In such an instance, we would be formally disobedient, for we would be disobeying precisely because we were commanded to keep silence by the rule. Otherwise, our talking at the time of silence was not formal disobedience but a circumstance accompanying our act of talking. True, it happened to be against the rule, and in that sense it was material disobedience, but that was not why we talked, and hence we were not formally disobedient.

Such disobedience in general is usually a symptom of some more serious disease. Something else lies hidden beneath it; the reason we talked was not disobedience; it was something else. We were proud, perhaps, or gave in to human respect, or were unmortified, or undisciplined. Therefore, we should not rest satisfied with merely confessing that we were disobedient, when we were not formally disobedient at all. We should find out what is causing us to break the rule. It is easier to say in confession: "I was disobedient to the rules three times," than it is to say, "I failed in silence because I was proud and arrogant," or, "because I gave in to human respect." To talk about a rash is not so embarrassing as talking about the disease that causes the rash.

Natural and Supernatural Obedience

We have said that when we do what we are commanded precisely because we are commanded, we have performed an act of the special virtue of obedience. But the special virtue of obedience can be either natural or supernatural. If someone does a thing because he has been commanded to do it, but has as his ultimate reason or motive merely some natural good, then he performs an act of the natural virtue of obedience. For example, if he carried out an order because he was commanded and because he knew it is necessary for good order, a natural and reasonable end, it would be an act of natural virtue. A soldier obeys the commands of his superior officer because he is told, and in order to win the war. If that is his ultimate intention, then he is practicing the natural virtue of obedience. A citizen undertaking jury duty because he has been commanded by the chief executive of the state is practicing the natural virtue of obedience, if he is doing it for the reason that it is necessary in order to achieve the good order of the state.

But, if one in the state of grace changes that natural motive to one which is supernatural, then he performs an act of supernatural special virtue of obedience. It consists in doing what we are commanded by lawful superiors precisely because we are commanded and ultimately *because it is God commanding us*, and because we know that all authority is from God, and he who resists the authority, resists the ordinances of God. Only in those circumstances do we practice the special supernatural virtue of obedience to lawful superiors of which Saint Thomas speaks.

Who, then, are our lawful superiors? Lawful superiors include officials of the Church, of the state, the family, the school, or place of work, depending upon the state of life in which we find ourselves. "There exists no authority except from God . . . he who resists the authority," says Saint Paul, "resists the ordinance of God; and they that resist bring on themselves condemnation."

Therefore, God's will is manifested to a professional football player through the coach, for all authority is from God, even the authority of a football coach over his players. God's will is manifested to a workman through the superintendent or the boss. As long as one freely places himself in a particular situation of life, then God manifests His will for him through the authority in that situation, in all that pertains to his duty and is not sinful.

Therefore, in regard to the laws of the Church, we are bound by obedience to observe the Code of Canon Law, all the precepts of the Church, the legislation concerning the rubrics, the liturgical laws, the teachings of our Holy Father as shown in the encyclicals and elsewhere, the pronouncements of our bishops and pastors and confessors and directors.

Under the authority of the State are included federal laws, state laws, county laws, municipal laws which we must obey. In the religious life, the supernatural familial society, taking the place of parental authority of the family, there is the authority of religious superiors. Therefore, we owe obedience to superiors as well as to the rules, the customs, the constitutions. But there are various grades of superiors. They range from the Pope down through the Superior General, the provincial superiors, and local superiors. We owe obedience to them all.

In addition, we owe obedience to subordinate authorities.

For example, when we are in the library, we owe obedience to the librarian. If the librarian tells us not to take certain books out because they are on the reference list, or reserve list, and should not be removed, obedience obliges us to comply. All authority, then, is from God, and obedience is a supernatural virtue which inclines us to submit our will to this authority precisely because we have been commanded, and because ultimately God himself is commanding us.

God Speaks through Human Instruments

The word obedience comes from *ob* and *audire* meaning "to hear." It has to do with hearing: Hearing the word of God, hearing the voice of God through some instrument He uses. There are many instruments in life through which we hear the voice of another. For example, the telephone, the radio, television, books; all these are media through which another's voice comes to us. God also makes His will known to us through human instruments which we call superiors or legitimate authorities. Through those instruments, we can "ob audire," we can hear God's voice, listen to it, and obey it. Obedience demands listening for the voice of God, independently of the kind of instrument which transmits it to us. It makes no difference whether we hear God's message from a telephone, a telegraph, or television, or a living human voice, whether it be manifested by a word, a glance, a nod, or frown. What we must listen to is the voice of God, coming to us through superiors.

This, of course, does not at all mean that we have to like our superiors in a natural way. It does not mean that we have to admire them; nor does it imply that we have to look up to them for their virtue or their learning; it means only that we must regard them as instruments which God uses to manifest His will to us. They are not, perhaps, the instruments we would choose ourself; but they are the ones God has chosen to represent Him.

We may see external imperfections in them, just as we might possibly see imperfections in the bread that becomes the Body of Christ in the Mass; but that does not affect in any way the results of the trans-substantiation. Our eyes of faith see only the underlying *reality*, not discerning the external accidents. So, too, with obedience by faith we recognize only the underlying *reality* that God's voice is speaking through this person when he or she is telling us to do or not to do something.

Again, our ears may hear only the human voice of the superior. That human voice we hear might conceivably be rasping, overbearing, or unkind; but we know it is God's voice speaking to us. Our ears of faith listen to the voice of God no matter how imperfect the medium through which it might come. We could listen to a radio or T.V. set which was out of adjustment, and the sound coming through might be garbled and filled with static. But as long as we can recognize the words, we would get the message. So, too, when we hear our superiors telling us to do or not to do, however distorted it may be by human considerations, we know we are hearing the message of God.

Thus, for the supernatural virtue of obedience to come into play, two wills must be involved: First of all, the will of the lawful superior made manifest in some way, either by writing or vocally, expressed or implied or tacit. Secondly, to that will, the Religious must submit his will by doing the thing commanded precisely because of his being commanded and because ultimately God is commanding him.

The will of a superior can be expressed in many ways. It can be merely tacit, but understood, without the superior saying anything. It can be manifested violently. The will of a superior can be expressed indifferently. For example, a Religious could ask if she might do such and such a thing.

The superior could answer: "Well, if you like, that will be all right; go ahead." Or again, the superior might say, "Do what you want about it." If a superior answers that way, then, whatever one prudently does is God's will in the matter, because the will of the superior is that the subject make her own decision. Thus, there are many ways the command or the will of a superior can be expressed or known in order to be the object of the virtue of obedience.

Furthermore, it makes no difference whether the will of the superior for us be just or unjust. As long as it is not sinful, we can exercise the virtue of obedience in fulfilling it. Our Divine Lord Himself obeyed unjust commands. Therefore, the justice or injustice, the comfortableness or agreeableness of the command, as long as it is not sinful, has no influence on the practice of the virtue of obedience, except, perhaps, to make it more meritorious. Even if a superior were unbelievably to indulge her unfairness on us, and say, "Stay there on your knees in the corner for an hour," that command could be the object of an act of the virtue of obedience. Even if a superior were actually to commit a sin in telling us to do something, being unkind or prejudiced in giving the command, we could still practice the virtue of obedience by carrying out her command if we have the proper motive. She represents God, and that is how He wants His will to come to us in that instance. Thus the superior's sin would not affect our virtuous act one iota.

A Virtual Intention Suffices

It is hardly necessary to say that in practicing the virtue of obedience the *intention* to do what we are told precisely because we are told, because ultimately it is God commanding us, need not be an *actual* intention. There are two kinds of intentions: Actual and virtual. An actual intention is one which exists here and now in us, and which is causing our action, and of which we are at the moment conscious. For example, if the superior told us to do an errand, and if we made the intention to do it from a motive of obedience, and while doing the errand we adverted to the fact that we were doing it because of supernatural obedience, that would be an actual intention.

Fortunately, theologians tell us we do not need an *actual* supernatural intention in order to gain the merit of our action. A *virtual* intention suffices. Virtual comes from the word "virtus" meaning strength; and a virtual intention is one, the strength of which flows into our action even though we are not conscious of it at the moment. A virtual intention is one we once made, did not retract, and which is causing in some way our action here, even though we do not advert to it or think of it.

For example, suppose we intended to walk to town to go to confession. On the way, we might stop at three or four stores. We might not be thinking at the time of going to confession at all. But our intention was to go to confession, and going to confession was influencing every step we took, every place we turned into. If anybody said to us, "Do you want to take a ride?", we would say, "No, I am going to confession." Right away, our intention would come back to us; we would recall what we were doing and why we were doing it. So, while we are not adverting to our intention, it is virtual if it is flowing into or causing our actions at every moment, even though we are not conscious of it.

A virtual intention, then, is sufficient to specify and preserve the merit of our virtuous actions. Such a virtual intention lasts and influences and gives value to our actions, theoretically at least, until it is retracted. But it is retracted in effect in any given instance by acting for a contrary motive. For example, the day we were confirmed, we made an intention of offering everything to God. Therefore, presumably, for the rest of our life, everything we do is for God.

But is it? On account of the vascillation of our human will, we have to renew that intention often. We can start out working to please God and end up in the completely opposite course of working to please ourself. Once we do anything to please self instead of God, we have vitiated our good motive and the virtual intention, at least in that instance.*

The Importance of Intention

The ideal, of course, is to have an actual intention as long as and as often as we perform an act of virtue. But we must be reconciled to the fact that this is impossible at every moment of our lives. However, it is an achievable goal to have an actual intention at least at the beginning of each of our main actions. It is possible to make an actual intention to do what we do for such and such a motive or motives before we start the action. But having made it, depending upon the nature of the work, almost immediately that actual intention would have to become virtual to permit us to put our mind to the work at hand. But renewing our actual intention from time to time during the action makes the virtual intention all the stronger. Further, it helps us develop the spirit of recollection and mental union with God as much as we can.

Therefore, intention is a vital factor in our spiritual life. Consequently, we should make an actual intention each morning, which will become a virtual intention throughout the day, to do all we are commanded precisely because we are commanded and because ultimately it is God commanding us. That is the intention necessary to practice the special virtue of obedience, and to make all our daily actions have the special merit of that virtue.

---

* Cf. Chapter 12, on Purity of Intention.

But before the virtue of obedience can be manifested externally as a habit, it must proceed from a pre-existing, interior disposition of the will. This disposition is essentially a desire and willingness to be told what to do. It is a deliberately willed subjection of one's self to another. To live a life of obedience fruitfully, necessarily means we must have that *spirit of obedience*, the spirit of wanting to be told at every moment what to do.

It is said that obedience is the grave where self-will is buried. But obedience puts self-will to death not sadistically, but only that it might do what God wants instead. It is a child-like, docile attitude toward God our Father. An obedient little child, a rare commodity in these days, seeks to find out before it goes up the street what its mother's will is. It goes into the house to ask mother if it may go here, if it may go there; if it may do this, or if it may do that.

A truly obedient Religious has that same spirit, that same child-like attitude toward God our Father. It is far from the discipline of a soldier which, no matter how well inculcated, is not necessarily the virtue of obedience. True, his carrying out of orders can be a virtue, if the soldier does what he is told because he is told, for the sake of the common good, or the survival of the commonweal, or because God is represented by his superior officers; but is not necessarily the virtue of obedience. Habitual acts of the virtue of obedience pre-suppose an interior spirit of wanting to be told what to do, which, in turn, flows from humility.

The Spirit of Independence

The spirit of obedience flows from the humble, absolute divesting of one's self of the opposite *spirit of independence*. Such a spirit is manifested by those who boast of knowing how to get their own will. They say: "I know what to do. I was not born yesterday; I've been around and can take care of myself." Such a spirit of independence is completely foreign to the true, humble, child-like spirit of obedience which wants to find out at every moment of life what God wants us to do. Those with the spirit of independence go through a kind of outward compliance with what they are told to do, from a certain sense of expediency. But while they comply outwardly, they maintain their integrity inviolate, shielded high up in their own ivory tower of independence.

They preserve their own will, their own personality intact by never really submitting it. They look upon having to do what they are told as a kind of belittling and unavoidable inconvenience that simply has to be gone through in religion. Being ordered by others is a liability they will have to put up with all their lives. They bristle each time they are told what to do, when they know so much better what they want to do or think they should do or feel like doing. They are obliged to submit in order to live community life. But come what may, their spirit of independence will defend the impregnable fortress of their own personality and will into which no one can penetrate. They think to themselves, perhaps even unconsciously: "I'll go through the external motions of doing what I am told, and I'll do enough to get by. But the dominating influence of my life will be myself, my own will, my own independence. I'll see to it that no one will push me where I don't want to go."

How foreign all such thinking is to the real spirit of obedience, that abiding desire to discover what God wants for us really and sincerely and honestly. It is a desire not to deceive ourselves, not to influence superiors to tell us what we want to do. It is a real, humble, child-like spirit and interior disposition to find out what God actually does want us to do at every moment. How opposed is such a spirit to scheming to get our own way, at the same time lulling ourselves into thinking that, because we go through the external motions, we are practicing the virtue of obedience while we somehow maintain that impregnable fortress of our own independence within us.

Such is not the virtue of obedience which makes every act we do under its domination an act of worship of God. We cannot have this spirit of obedience and be stiff-necked and proud as Christ said the scribes and Pharisees were. We have to bend down, to stoop low; we have to be humble. Yet, what apparently contradictory results! "The foolish things of this world has God chosen to put to shame the wise." "For everyone who exalts himself shall be humbled, and he who humbles himself shall be exalted." To bend down low, to be anxious, solicitous, zealous to find out what God wants us to do is the most ennobling habit we can have.

The Nobility of Obedience

The highest operation possible to our God-given faculty of *intellect* is to use it to find God and His will so that we may do it. The greatest use to which we can apply our human *will* is to conform it to God's will by obeying it. Thus, acts of the virtue of obedience are the noblest, most elevating, most heroic, most meritorious and praiseworthy operations we can perform with our human nature, because we thereby devote it most completely to its highest object which is God, who constitutes its ultimate end and happiness. There is nothing debasing about obedience, nothing subservient, nothing crawling, nothing humbling, if we see reality as it is through God's eyes, if we use our supernatural gift of faith to see things as they are. Only the maxims of the world can make obedience appear humbling. Only the maxims of the world can make pride and independence and arrogance appear something to be admired; but that is not reality.

Reality is things as they are in the actual order God has

established. True greatness, seen through the eyes of God, true holiness, true sanctity, than which there is none greater, is this: Constantly and always to have the disposition of trying to find out what God wants. We find out what He wants through the rules, the customs, the constitutions of our community, the voice of superiors, those with whom we work, our companions.

To realize the extent to which the virtue of obedience can be developed, we have but to read the lives of the saints. They loved to look for God's will in every situation of life, even in recreation. They loved to let God's will be expressed for them through somebody else's will. To their companions they would look for the answers to such questions as: "What shall we do today? What shall we talk about? What shall we play? Where shall we go for a walk?" They wanted, even in such simple things as these, to look for a manifestation of God's will and to do it in the spirit of obedience, lest they strengthen self-will by doing it even one more time. To find out from their fellow man, even though equals and subordinates, what God's will was for them was their goal.

They realized that the one, the only, the greatest obstacle to sanctification, the obstacle that obstructs the fulfilling of the purpose of existence, that stands between our perfection and us, that stands between God and us is our *own will*. They knew, further, that the virtue of obedience is the virtue par-exellence to put self-will to death. This attitude of obedience was folly to the Greeks and a stumbling block to the Jews, for it was contrary to the maxims of the world. To submit one's will to another was the mark of a snivelling sychophant or grovelling slave.

Such a view results from looking through the wrong end of the telescope. It makes one person doing the will of another appear small and tiny and insignificant. But such is not the virtue of obedience. Reversing the telescope gives the realistic view and shows the enlarged and increased stature of one person doing the will of another because that other represents God, and thus the person is only doing God's will. It shows him using his human faculties for the most ennobling, sanctifying, perfecting end possible, the end the pagan philosophers fought for years to discover, namely to unite it with God. Those philosophers could not dream there could be such a thing as supernatural obedience, because it is beyond the power of human reason to know, and can be known only by our infused faculty of knowing with the knowledge of God which is called faith.

The Folly and Ruin of Independence

Behold the splendor of the virtue of obedience! Behold the folly of independence; the folly of our rearing up like Lucifer and saying to God, "I will not serve. I am not interested in doing Your will. I am not interested in finding out what Your will is. I want to do my own will. I may have to conform externally to what I am told to do, but my will shall prevail eventually; wait and see." What folly, what stupidity, what waste of talents, what waste of faculties, what destruction of human things that are noble and beautiful and sacred!

In his book, *In The Steps of The Master*, H. V. Morton gives a description of a ruined house in the district of Caesarea-Phillipi which conveys some of the horror of wasted powers and gifts. He says in describing the house:

It is a confused mass of stone, nearly all of it Roman. Built into the walls, not upright but in a parallel position, are dozens of lovely marble columns. At first it looks as though the place is built of round stones. Then one realizes that these are the bases of columns. There is something positively sickening in the sight of it. One sees in imagination the onrush of barbarians, the frightful destruction of beauty and the blind ignorant rebuilding by a savage race. When the Roman empire fell, towns like Caesarea-Phillipi became stone quarries. One can see so clearly how a statue by Phydias could be hacked to pieces to be put into the walls of a hovel. We all know that these things happen, but the sight of one building, with altars and inscriptions built into its walls and Corinthian columns used to support floors instead of roofs seems to bring home more vividly than any chapter by Gibbon the horror that attends the extinction of a culture." [1]

Such is the ruin wrought in our super nature by the spirit of independence. It is an ignorant, barbaric, worldly destruction and misuse of our noble, God-given faculties of intellect and will, refusing to devote them to the use for which they were made and given to us. In another place in his book Mr. Morton says: "Nothing, I think, is more depressing than the sight of uncivilized people living in squalor amid the ruins of something that has once been noble." [2] To which one might add, more depressing still is the sight of human faculties of intellect and will, supernaturalized by faith and charity, being savagely squandered and misused in independence when they were made to be used so nobly in obedience. By such mis-use, we *oppose* God with our faculties, instead of serving Him with them. On the other hand, the greatest use of them we can make is to conform them to the divine will as made known through God's human representative, namely, authority.

In order, then, to have an act of the supernatural virtue of obedience, it is necessary to do what we are told, precisely because we are told, and because ultimately the one telling us represents God. Consequently, we obey because God is telling us to do the thing. It is obvious that, in addition to or instead of that motive, we could possibly have one or

---

[1] Page 274.
[2] *Ibid.*, page 295.

several other motives for doing what we do, motives that would not constitute the virtue of obedience.

False Motives for Obedience

Consider for a moment some of the more well known possible motives we might have for doing what we were told:

We might like the thing we're told to do or we might like the person who tells us to do it;

We might do the thing in order to be thought well of;

We might do it in order to keep the peace;

We might do it because we fear the consequences if we don't do it;

We might do what we are told merely for the sake of getting the thing done; because it is easier to do it than to plan our own activity;

We might do what we are told in order that we might succeed in our duty;

We might do it from a motive of human respect;

We might do it from pride of accomplishment;

We might do it because we liked the way we were asked to do it;

We might do it because someone will talk about us if we do it, or if we do not do it;

We might do it because somebody will praise us for doing it;

We might do it because it happens to be convenient;

We might do it to please somebody;

We might do it to get a promotion;

We might do it because we are naturally submissive and docile and don't like to oppose anyone.

In addition to these, many other motives could possibly induce us to do what we are told. But *not one* of these motives is sufficient for an act of the supernatural virtue of obedience! To do what we are told to do to please a superior, so that people will think well of us, so that we will get a good reputation, so we'll get the thing done, because of the consequences, to keep the peace, to be thought well of, because we like the superior, because we like the way she tells us to do a thing, because she is always so gracious, because it is a pleasure to do something for her, because she always does something in return; to do what we are told because of the unpleasant consequences otherwise, to do it out of human respect, because we're ashamed not to do it, because we'll be thought poorly of if we don't do it—if *any* of these is our motive for doing what we are told, we are *not* practicing the supernatural virtue of obedience!

Our motive must be *supernatural,* and none of the false motives mentioned is supernatural. They can all be categorized by saying that our motive for obedience must not be so we will *feel* good, or so we will *look* good, but so that we will *be* good. The only motive that constitutes the supernatural virtue of obedience is this: That God is commanding us.

An Interesting Speculation

An interesting speculation presents itself at this point. It has been said that if we submit our will and do what we are told without any particular motive, or for some natural or bad motive, we do not have, according to Saint Thomas, the supernatural virtue of obedience. That is present only when we do what we do precisely because we have been told to do it, and because ultimately God is telling us to do it.

Remembering this fact, the interesting speculation runs thus: Would it be possible for Religious to go through their whole religious life doing what they were told, but without ever really practicing the supernatural virtue of obedience because of a lack of proper motive? Would it be possible for them to go along, conforming externally with regulations, doing what they are told because they want to get along with a minimum of friction?

They are told to teach, and they teach. They are told to go to a particular mission, and they go to that mission. When their mission is changed, they move to the new one. They get up in the morning and say all their morning prayers, and do all their spiritual exercises throughout the day. They do what they are told; they get into no trouble that way. They are striving to live in a community and do their work with a minimum of friction; they enjoy teaching, they enjoy nursing, or being good professional people. But they do what they are told from a motive of enlightened self-interest. They have been around a few years and know that the best way to get along is to conform, at least externally, and in that way they do not get themselves into any trouble. In other words, they lead a purely naturalistic kind of existence.

The question, then, is: Can there be such people? Is it possible for someone to go on living in religious life week after week, and month after month, without practicing the supernatural virtue of obedience, which means seeking to find out what God wants, wanting to find out what He wants, and doing it because it is His will, because He has commanded it? Is it possible to live habitually like that?

Is it possible to live long periods of time doing what we are told only because it seems right, or because it seems just, or because it seems reasonable or pleasant, or because it seems easy, or because we have to, or because we'll please those who tell us to do it, or because we like those who tell us to do it, or because we'll be a success if we do it, but never precisely because it is commanded and *it is what God wants,* even though it seems to be the most foolish thing in the world for us to do? Is it possible for people to live practically their whole religious life like that?

Our community periodically recalls this fearful possibility

to us. We are reminded in retreats of the nature of the virtues of our state, because we can fall by the wayside. We are reminded in meditations and instruction that it is perfectly possible to live religious life almost entirely on the first floor of sensuality. This is not to say that we never make an act of the virtue of obedience; but it means that by and large we can live habitually on the first floor of feelings with regard to the virtue of obedience, obeying only because we feel like it. Even the second floor of reason or common sense is not elevated enough to permit practice of the supernatural virtue of obedience. Its inhabitants obey because the command is just, because it seems right or reasonable.

Universal, Entire, Prompt Obedience

On the third floor of faith, we obey solely because *God manifests His will* to us in this command, in this custom, this rule, this precept, this thing we are asked to do, this thing we are told not to do, this appointment posted on the board, this change of duty, this mission, this office, this study we have to do at this hour, this work we have to do at this time. We do what He wants because He wants it, and are grateful to Him for letting us know so clearly what He wants us to do. Such is the supernatural virtue of obedience. Is it possible to live long periods of time without practicing it?

In addition to being supernatural the virtue of obedience must be *universal* in extent. That is, it must extend to all the commands of legitimate superiors. We cannot select and choose among the commandments of lawful superiors as to which we will obey and which we will not. We can not say: "I will do everything you tell me to do, except this." If the superior has the right to tell us to do even one thing within his competency, he has a right to tell us to do this particular thing. Eliminating any individual command would overthrow the very foundations of supernatural obedience.

For the only possible reason for eliminating any one command, or group of commands, would be that in regard to that one particular command or in that group of commands, the superior, for some reason, was not God's representative. But if in A and B and C and D, the superior is God's representative, then he has to be God's representative in E and F and G and H and I. If a superior is God's representative at all, then he expresses God's will in everything within his competency.

In addition to supernatural obedience being universal in extent, it must also be *entire* in execution. This means we must carry out the entire command of any superior. We must do all the superior says, not just half of it. Again, this conclusion follows from the very nature of obedience, for if a command is God's will, then every part of the command is likewise His will.

Furthermore, obedience demands that we do *promptly* what we are commanded. If lawful superiors tell us they want something done, the presumption is they have a time limit during which they want it done. Prompt obedience implies that we do it at that time or within that time. Therefore, if we procrastinate two or three days or a week, obviously we are not showing much enthusiasm for doing the will of another. Consequently, we demonstrate that our motive is not correct; we show we are not happy to do God's will, but our own, for the will of the superior also includes the time they want their request fulfilled.

Cheerful Obedience

A final quality supernatural obedience should have, according to spiritual writers and theologians, is *cheerfulness*. If we fail to do the will of the superior cheerfully, we indicate that we lack the spirit of obedience, that we are not seeing the superior's will as God's will, and consequently have the wrong motive. If we do what we are told to do because it is the definite, signified will of God, we will do it cheerfully.

But doing God's will cheerfully does not mean that we *feel* like doing it. Contrary feelings do not at all vitiate the supernatural intention or motive we have in doing what we are told to do.

We need not suppose that our Divine Lord was cheerful the night that He went through the agony in the Garden and faced the morrow fearfully. We could hardly think He was cheerful in the sense that word normally conveys. We know surely He was not singing. As a matter of fact, He was praying over and over that He would not have to go through the awful trial ahead. "Father, if it be possible, let this chalice pass from me. Nevertheless not as I will, but as thou wilt." In that final phrase, we find the exemplification of cheerful obedience. It means cheerful acceptance of His Father's will.

To be sure, cheerful seems a rather strange adjective to modify the word obedience. Actually, its meaning here more accurately opposes rebelling or reluctant obedience. Rebellious or reluctant obedience, the opposite of cheerful in this sense, would most likely appear in difficult things we are asked to do. If we have listened with faith to the voice of God coming to us through some instrument, whether the instrument be a book, a human voice, or a letter, we are anxious to do all that God has commanded us, and because it is God's will, we try to do it cheerfully in spite of our feelings to the contrary. When we get an unpleasant message of obedience, we should pray to be delivered from the temptation to be rebellious or reluctant, instead of cheerful.

This is particularly important to remember when we are on a mission, or in a duty about which everything is a cross and a trial. We can be tempted to make up our mind to keep at it for just so long. We can soliloquize: "I can't stand this thing another month. I'm going to ask for a change. I can't go on. I've got to get out of it someway. I'll tell them I'm sick. I'll tell them I can't do it. Nobody should be expected to do this."

Sometimes such apparent frustration may be all in our head, a subtle escape mechanism to evade a difficult situation. On the other hand, it may have a foundation in reality. If we represent the problem to superiors, and God manifests His will to be that we keep on doing the same thing, then we must continue as long as God wills. He will give us the strength to do so.

We can not set any predetermined limit to our patience or our desire to conform our will to God's will without rebelling. If we say: "I will do it for so long, but there will come a point after which I will not," there is something wrong with our supernatural motive. The spirit of obedience necessarily means wishing to do not only what the superior says, but also when the superior says it, and in the way the superior says it, and *as long as the superior wants,* because it is commanded, and because it is God commanding it, therefore it is God's will.

Obedience and Sacrifice

Realizing this, we can understand better what God meant when He said in the Scriptures: "Obedience is better than sacrifices." A sacrifice is essentially an external *sign* instituted by God and indicating that those who are taking part in the offering of it have submitted their will to God. It is a sign of submission or conformity of our will to God's will. On the other hand, obedience is *more than a sign* of submission. It is an *actual submission,* an actual conformity of our will to God's will. Therefore, it is a better thing than sacrifice, for a thing itself is always better than its symbol. It is better to have cash in our hand than a promissory note signifying cash. A sacrifice is kind of a promissory note saying to God: "I will submit my will to You, You wait and see, dear God." But obedience is the actual submission; therefore obedience is better than sacrifice.

In brief summary, we have seen thus far that the special virtue of obedience is distinguished by its *motive* from the circumstance of obedience which accompanies the fulfilling of any law. To practice the special virtue of obedience, we must obey precisely for this motive: That we have been commanded and because ultimately we are commanded by God. The essence of the virtue of obedience is submission of the will for that motive.

Obedience of Judgement

But there is another phase of obedience which looms large in the works of every master of the spiritual life. It is called obedience of the *judgement*. It is imperative that we understand both parts of the thesis which states that the perfection of obedience consists of two elements: submission of the will, and submission of the judgement. Perhaps no element of the virtue of obedience causes more concern to well-intentioned Religious than the concept of submission of the judgement.

First of all, it is obvious that the thing to which we must submit our judgement is the command of the superior. But what does it mean to submit our judgement? Does it mean keeping our opinion to ourself? Does it mean not having an opinion? Does it mean not making a judgement? No! All this is *not* doing something; it is *not* judging. On the contrary, if we must *submit* our *judgement,* we obviously have to *make* a judgement. And that is precisely what we are called upon to do, namely, make a submissive judgement.

But does submission of our judgement mean that we have to do violence to our intellect? Does it mean that, if a superior tells us to put on our shawl because it is cold out, we have to judge we need the shawl, when, in fact, we do not? Does submitting our judgement mean we have to think it is cold; that we need a shawl when obviously the sun is shining and it is warm?

Not at all! It can not. There must be some other answer. The command is to wear our shawl. We submit our *will*, by wearing the shawl. But what precisely do we do with our *judgement* when we submit it?

A judgement is a comparison of two ideas. The first part of the judgement in question, the first idea, is the command the superior has given us. We are to make a judgement about that command. What are we to judge about it? To submit our judgement means that we will finish ultimately with the same kind of judgement the superior made, namely, that this command or prohibition is the best thing for us.

The supposition is that the superior tells us to wear our shawl going over to the school. What does our reason force us to say about this command? A look at the thermometer indicates that it is not the best thing to do objectively. We don't need the shawl, obviously. Why go to all the trouble of getting it out and putting it on? We were just going to run over to school and run right back, and we'll have to take it off again and fold it up.

But the superior has said, "Wear your shawl." When she says that, God is saying it, and faith tells us, therefore, that this command must be the best thing to do. But how can we reconcile that with what our reason tells us? How can we *submit* our judgement, which seems to require doing violence to our intellect and the evidence of our senses?

Objective and Subjective Judgements

In order to resolve the dilemma and make sense out of the

practice of submission of the judgement, we must make a very important distinction between two kinds of judgements: objective and subjective judgements. An objective judgement considers a thing as it is *in itself*, independently of us, or its relation to us, or its influence or effect on us. For example, take the proposition of wearing a shawl as we have been told to do. If, independently of whether we want to or feel like wearing it, we try to judge whether anybody *needs* a shawl today, such a judgement would be considering the proposition *objectively*, as it is in itself. We try honestly to take ourselves out of the picture and judge the thing as it is in itself.

But when we consider or judge a proposition *subjectively*, we consider it insofar *as it affects us*. We consider the thing in relation to ourselves; we are the subject concerned.

Here we are at the crux of the problem. When there is question of submission of our judgement, we are concerned *only with subjective judgements*. Let that be noted carefully. Obedience of the judgement has to do *only with subjective judgements*. That is, we are obliged to judge a command only *insofar as it affects us*, and not as it is objectively in itself.

So, then, to return to our example of being told to wear our shawl: Objectively, is the shawl needed today? For the sake of our discussion, we can presume that it definitely is *not* needed, that to wear it is *not* the best thing. But submitting our judgement means, very plainly, that we judge it as the best thing *for us* to wear that shawl *today* because we have been commanded by lawful authority, and that authority speaks for God; therefore God is commanding us. Consequently, *for us, in this instance*, the best thing is to wear the shawl. *That* is submission of the judgement. But note well that it is completely independent of what our *objective* judgement might be about this matter.

As a further illustration, suppose we are told to teach

a certain class, or undertake a certain duty; it does not seem to us the best thing to do, objectively speaking; it does not seem the best way or the best time to do it. But no matter what we may judge of that command objectively and in itself, we submit our judgement whenever we judge that it is the best thing *for us* to do here and now. Why? Because we have been told to do it by authority, and that is God telling us to do it; therefore, *for us,* it is the *best* thing to do, no matter how unwise it might appear objectively.

Therefore, we must be aware that submission of judgement does not at all mean that we refrain from judging. It is not negative. Submission of the judgement means we do judge.

In summary, then, submission of the judgement means this: we judge subjectively that the command we receive is the best thing for us to do here and now, because it is God's will for us, independently of what it may be objectively or what we may think of its wisdom or timeliness objectively. This is most necessary, especially when, with our puny mind, we can not see why it is the best thing for us to do. Our faith tells us that it is God's will, and He knows what is best for us in order that He might work out His plan in us. He is all wise, and He knows what is best for us; He is all good and wants what is best for us; He is all powerful, and will do what is best for us, even though we can not see how it is best for us.

If we have the spirit of obedience, we judge thus spontaneously, automatically, so to speak. Such is the habit of submission of the judgement. Such a habit is possible and most meritorious even in situations in which we think that objectively the command is *not* the best thing to do, or it is not the best time to do it. If we have the habit of submission of judgement, we strive to avoid judging whether a command is objectively right or not. That is a mark of the spirit of independence. We immediately think only that we have been told by God's representative and therefore, it is the right thing *for us*. Our spontaneous reaction to any command will be: "No matter what it seems like to me, I know this is the right thing for me to do because God is commanding me."

Objective and Subjective Judgements May Differ

As has been said, submission of the judgement does not militate against our knowing that, humanly speaking, what we are told to do seems not to be the best thing to do. Recall the example in Rodriguez of the novice who watered a dry stick because the superior had told him to do so. At the superior's behest he stuck a dry stick in the ground and kept watering the dry piece of dead wood, day after day, from a spirit of obedience. Eventually, it blossomed! God rewarded his virtue of obedience by visible signs.

We can imagine the objections that occurred to him when he heard the command, "Water this stick." Would not his obvious judgement be that this command was certainly not the best thing to do? But submission of his judgement for him was to judge it was the best thing for him to do because God was commanding it. Sometimes, we who receive commands think, in the pride of our own conceit, that we know what is right and best to do, and then God has a way of straightening us out.

It is deserving of notice that submission of judgement applies not alone to specific commands of superiors; it is likewise necessary for obedience to any custom, or rule, or any one of the constitutions. It may not seem quite wise to us; it may not seem the best; there may not seem to be much sense in it; but none of these objections has anything

to do with real obedience. The virtue of obedience requires that we *submit* our will and judgement; and submission of our judgement means that whatever it may be
objectively, we judge that rule or custom or constitution
is the best thing for us because it is God's will for us.

Importance of Submission of Judgement

Actually, it is difficult to see how there can be any virtue
of obedience at all without submission of our judgement.
If the virtue of obedience means acting because we are
commanded and because ultimately we are commanded
by God, how can we withhold submission of our judgement? How can we say, "This is not the best thing for me
to do because God does not know what He is doing when
He commands me thus." Failure to submit our judgement
implies just that. But how can we think that God is telling
us to do something that is not best for us in the light of
His purpose? How can we obey because God is commanding us, and not submit our judgement to the command?
If we believe God is commanding us, how can we fail to
judge that it is the best thing for us to do here and now?

On the other hand, if we strive for submission of judgement, as we advance toward the perfection of obedience,
even the struggle against our *objective* judgement will les-
sen. We approach more and more the obedience of our
Divine Lord who became obedient unto death to redeem
man. Disobedience was the cause of man's fall, and obedience saved him, the submission of the will and judgement
of the Son of God to God the Father. If Christ had merely
died, without submitting His judgement to God, rebelling
against His Father's will, we would not have been saved.
Only because He willingly accepted death in conformity
to the will of the Father did He merit heaven for us. He

need not have judged objectively that His death was the best thing. But He judged that subjectively the best thing for Him in those circumstances was to die in conformity with the will of His Father. Thus, He said: "For this reason the Father loves me, because I lay down my life that I may take it up again. No one takes it from me, but I lay it down of myself. I have the power to lay it down, and I have the power to take it up again. Such is the command I have received from my Father." He submitted His will and His judgement completely. He is our model if we are to advance in the practice of the virtue of obedience, without which we might as well forget the religious life and community life, for its essence is the spirit of obedience which implies the submission of our will and judgement.

Obedience Is Reasonable

Let it be emphasized that such submission of will and judgement to that of superiors as representatives of God is eminently *reasonable*. A little novice, in explaining the virtue of obedience at one time, said, "If we are reasoning things out, we can't have the virtue of obedience." Such a statement is, of course, utterly false and a grotesque distortion of the truth. Obedience, as is every part of the religious life, is completely reasonable. It *must be* since religious life is the highest and most perfect state of life on earth. Therefore, there *cannot* be anything in it that would militate against the highest development of all our faculties, and, above all, the highest faculties that we have, namely our intellect and will.

God gave us these faculties to *use* to glorify Him and thus perfect ourselves. And we use our intellect and will *most perfectly* when we use them to glorify God by having them united with His mind and will. But, to have our mind and will most perfectly united to that of God is but another way of defining the virtue of obedience. In practicing the virtue of obedience, we are, in fact, devoting our mind and will to the greatest purpose for which they could possibly be used. Consequently, there is *nothing* about the virtue of obedience that is debasing or stultifying or atrophying to our most noble faculties of mind and will. Let it never be for a moment admitted or thought that there is. And let the virtue of obedience never be explained to anyone in such a way as to leave the impression that there might be!

The only way one could conclude that the virtue of obedience is unreasonable, or that it demands violence to or misuse or disuse of our minds, would be by reasoning from wrong premises, from the maxims of the world and pride instead of from the maxims of Christ and faith. Begin the reasoning process with *reality as it is:* the greatest, most reasonable and noblest use to which a creature can devote his mind and will is to unite them with God's mind and will. Compare with that premise the minor that nowhere do we unite our minds and will so closely and perfectly with God's mind and will as in practicing the virtue of obedience. We thus come up with the inexorable conclusion that the greatest and most reasonable use to which we can devote our minds and wills is to practice the virtue of obedience.

So, anathema to all such false, misleading, degrading statements as that which says that if we are reasoning things out, we cannot be practicing the virtue of obedience. The fact is that *only on condition* that we *are* reasoning things out from the proper premises, only on condition that we *are reasonable* can we practice the true virtue of obedience, which is the *most reasonable* line of conduct that a person can follow on earth, namely, to be guided and moved toward perfection at every moment of life by Almighty God Himself through His human instruments. "For whoever are led by the Spirit of God, they are the sons of God."

Superiors Are Obliged to Obedience

Needless to say, all that has been said about obedience applies to every Religious without exception, and not just to those who are referred to as subjects. All Religious are not divided into two strata with a sharp line of demarcation drawn at the level between subjects and local superiors, so that those below the line are bound by obedience, while all those above the line are at liberty to lead a blissfully free existence of doing their own will, exempt from obedience.

The very same obligation of obedience which binds subjects in relation to local superiors also binds local superiors in relation to provincial superiors, and provincial superiors in relation to general superiors, and general superiors in relation to the Holy See. If anything, superiors have a graver obligation to submit their will and judgement to higher superiors by reason of the example they are held to give to those whom they rule. Superiors at any level of authority fail more seriously by rebellion or criticism or murmuring or lack of submission of will and judgement to their own superiors than do those who do not hold their responsibilities, and who do not have their grace of office to realize the importance of obedience and the devastation brought by disobedience.

All this, of course, is not to deny the difficulty, humanly and naturally speaking, of submitting our judgement. We find it hard because we are so used to judging things for ourselves; we are so accustomed to want to see why, to want to know why. We have been so schooled to fight our way in the world, to be masters of our own decisions, that when we attempt to turn ourselves over completely to God, we have to fight all those ingrained tendencies. We are attached to our own judgement, not because it is so right, but because we think it is so right, and because we are so used to living by it.

Obedience Is Childlike

On the other hand, those who have developed the true spirit of obedience, who have overcome their habit of living by maxims of the world, are so anxious to hear the voice of God coming to them through superiors, the rules, customs and constitutions, that they customarily ignore completely their objective judgement about the rightness or wrongness of a command in itself. They are interested only in what God wants them to do.

They have the spirit of a little child who does not ask itself whether it is best to go to the store, or to do the dishes, or do the errands that mother tells him to do. He knows mother wants it, so he does it. The child does not judge, he knows that he is not able to judge. The mother tells him: "Go over to Mrs. Smith with this note." The child goes over to Mrs. Smith with the note, and comes back with a cup full of sugar. He doesn't know and doesn't care about the wisdom of the command or whether it would be better to go later instead of now, whether it would be better to get salt instead of sugar, or whether it would be better to go to Mrs. Jones instead of to Mrs. Smith. Mother told him, and therefore he does what she tells him. "Unless you become as little children, you shall not enter the kingdom of heaven"; the spirit of obedience is such a child-like spirit.

CHAPTER VII

Why Be Obedient?

PERHAPS THE MOST obvious motive for devotion to the virtue of obedience is that there is no surer way of doing God's will than by practicing this virtue. We receive in the command of a superior a direct message in God's own voice or handwriting, as it were. When we are obedient, we know we are not doing our own will. We know we are not opposing God's will. Thus, if we really had faith and realized this, we would *rather* be told what to do than to decide what to do ourselves, for then we would be certain to do God's will.

Our Lord said one day to Saint Gertrude, "I will not ask an accounting of what anybody does under obedience; that accounting will be demanded of the superior. Those who do something from obedience will not have to account for *what* they do; they will only have to account to Me for the *way* they do it." Where could we find a more wonderful spiritual Blue Cross Plan, or health insurance? We might even call it fire insurance. As long as we do what God tells us to do through superiors, we never have to worry about *what* we are doing. Is there anything more consoling and reassuring than being told to do something by God?

People sometimes fear the judgement to come after death; but there's no reason to be afraid of the judgement when we are obedient. If God should say to us at the judgement: "Depart from me," we can say to Him, "You can't say that to me, dear God, for I did only what You told me to do through superiors. Therefore, I always did Your will." All we have to worry about or account for in obedience is the *way* we do what God has told us to do, which should be promptly, cheerfully, and with love.

Again, obedience is an excellent virtue because it participates in the virtue of religion which is the highest of the moral virtues. The virtue of religion is called the highest, the most excellent of the moral virtues, because it has as its object the very worship itself of God. In performing acts of religion, we are united directly with God.

Obedience and Worship of God

But the worship of our will, which is the worship of obedience, is almost directly connected with the virtue of religion. We *worship* God, practically speaking, when we unite our wills to His through the virtue of obedience as Christ did when, saying, "Not my will, but thine be done," He accepted death on the cross.

What, then, are some practical consequences of the fact that obedience is such an excellent virtue and partakes so much of the nature of the virtue of religion or the worship of God? Obviously, it is most salutary and beneficial and wise for us to do everything we possibly can with the intention of doing it because it is what God wants, or in other words, from a motive of obedience. We should try to make obedience a conscious motive in all of our actions. After doing things for the love of God, there is no greater motive for which to do them than this, that God has told us to do them; there is no better way to manifest our love of God than through the practice of obedience.

Because the virtue of obedience partakes of the nature of religion and worship of God, one not having the vow of obedience who does everything from the spirit of obedience thereby turns everything into a quasi act of religion. Thus, they make every thing they do an act of worship of God, as do those who have a vow of obedience, if their acts are influenced in any way by their vow. If, without vows, we do everything from a spirit of obedience, doing what we do because we are asked to do it and because ultimately God is asking us to do it, then everything becomes an act of the worship of God, whether it be carrying out rules, customs, constitutions, precepts, commandments of God or of the Church, or orders of superiors.

If we do that, are we not praying always, as our Lord told us to do? If prayer is the union of our mind and will with God, then obedience is prayer, for it means union of our will and judgement with God. Through it, our whole life becomes a kind of act of worship of God and prayer. Whenever we are obedient, it is as if we were praying, and we are fulfilling the command of God who told us to pray always.

This is true, of course, not only of religious obedience; the same result attaches to every obedience, whether we are a Sister, Brother, priest, or married, or single. Whenever we obey legitimate authority with the proper intention, we worship God. We must not make the mistake of thinking the virtue of obedience is reserved for the elite, for those who are in on secret knowledge. It is Christian doctrine that everyone can practice the virtue of obedience, that is, doing what they are told, not because it seems right to them, not because it seems reasonable, not because it seems sensible, not because they like the one they do it for, not because of the way they will be thanked, not because it makes them feel good, not because they know they can do a good job of it, not because they know they can make a name for themselves, not because they know they will get a promotion, but *because they are told* to do so, and ultimately because it is God telling them.

Thus, even if we do not have a vow of obedience, we can make our whole life an act of worship of God by practicing the virtue of obedience, doing what God wants us to do because He has asked us to do it.

Obedience and Charity

Actually, we have a further motive for the practice of the virtue of obedience in religious life in that we have an obligation to do so in *charity*. The superiors of a community take upon themselves the obligation to lead us and our companions to perfection, to form us, to protect us, and to direct us. When we fail to follow their direction by failing to submit our will and judgement to them, we are frustrating their efforts in our behalf. We, in effect, are challenging them to dare to try to do for us what we came and asked them to do. We are sabotaging their efforts, taking their time from other companions.

When we entered the novitiate, and with greater reason, when we accepted the habit of our community, we entered a society. No one forced us to do this. We entered freely and willingly. As a matter of fact, if we were forced to enter by any power on earth, whether fear, coercion, violence, or any other factor that could be construed as forcing us into the community, our entrance would be invalid. It would matter not that we had solemn, perpetual vows for forty years. In the supposition, not only our entry, but even our vows would be invalid.

Thus, we enter and remain in our religious society freely. When we do, we freely place ourselves under the authority of the superiors and voluntarily place ourselves under the scope of their power, giving over to them the right to determine our course of action. Therefore, we freely engage ourselves to practice obedience. In that voluntary oblation lies the glory of religious life. But if, any time, in any place or circumstance, we rebel against obedience, and refuse to submit our will and judgement, we are taking back to that extent the choice we made. There is rapine in our holocaust. We are telling God by our actions that we did not mean it when we gave ourselves over to superiors to make us perfect according to the spirit of our community. Having done that, we say in effect to them, "Now, go ahead and try to make me perfect; I dare you!" Consequently, from the point of view of charity, we have an obligation to practice the virtue of obedience, to submit our will and our judgement and not frustrate the efforts of superiors to lead us to holiness.

A Right to Correction

While speaking of the efforts of superiors to lead us to holiness, it would not be amiss to mention a point which is frequently obscured in the minds of Religious. As was said at the beginning of the treatment of obedience, when we enter religious life, we enter a society, which implies authority. Upon entrance, we acquire a *right* to be led along the road to perfection, the primary end of every community. The superiors of the community, to repeat, take upon themselves the responsibility of leading us along that road by providing the particular means available in our community, and in accordance with its particular spirit.

The obligations of the superiors, for which they will be responsible to God, are the same as the obligations of parents toward their children, namely, to instruct, correct, exercise vigilance over us, and to give us good example. Since that is the *obligation* of the authority, it follows that the Religious acquires a *right* to all those functions, namely, instruction, correction, vigilance, and example.

Thus, when we fail to conform to the prescripts of the Rules, or the orders of superiors, we do an injustice to our companions by sabotaging the proper functioning of the community and keep it from attaining its common end to a greater or lesser degree, however imperceptible it may be. As the poet has said, no man is an island, complete in himself, but each is part of the mainland. And no little part of the mainland is washed away into the sea without the whole being affected. So, the spirit of a community, and the amount of glory it gives to God, and the progress it makes toward achieving all of its ends is only the sum total of all those factors in its individual members. Thus, when one fails in obedience, at very least he deprives his companions of the good example to which they have a right. Hence, there devolves upon the superior the obligation to make a correction.

Now, it is important to note that it was said above that the Religious, when he enters a community, acquires a *right to correction* just as he receives a right to instruction, vigilance, and good example. This follows from the fact that he receives a right to be guided toward perfection. Not only does he acquire this right, but it should be noted that it is a particular kind of exclusive right, one of those inalienable rights which are not able to be taken away from one, and which one is not able himself to renounce because they pertain to the very nature of a state in life. It is something like the right one acquires upon entering the state of matrimony. When one marries, he must enter matrimony *as God established it,* and not according to some matrimonial arrangement he might devise himself for his own convenience. Otherwise, he does not enter marriage at all. When he does enter marriage, he acquires an exclusive right to the body of his partner, and vice versa. Matrimony, as God established it, is *one;* and no partner of a marriage can give over or give up to another his exclusive right to the body of his partner which he acquires in marriage, for this is of the very nature of the state of matrimony.

So, too, when one enters religious life, he enters it *as God has established it,* and not according to some arrangement he wishes to devise for himself. When he does enter, he acquires an *inalienable right* to correction. However much he might wish to relinquish that right, it is not within his power to do so, for it is of the very nature of the religious state. Corresponding to the right is a duty on the part of the superior to give the correction when it is needed.

Hence, the importance of having a correct attitude toward correction. Hence the importance of seeing correction in the spirit of faith and looking upon it as a directive from God Himself. Correction is *not* punishment, but merely a setting us back on the correct path to perfection, a process to which we acquired a right when we entered. Looking upon correction in this way will enable us to use it as God intended it to be used, namely as a means to greater love for Him, instead of making it a stumbling block of resentment and self-justification at imagined persecution on the part of the superior.

Obedience and Humility

In addition to the obligation from charity, there is a further obligation to practice the virtue of obedience from the point of view of *humility.* Being attached to our own will and our own judgement is a form of pride. It is pride to oppose the graces God gives those in office to carry out their duties and to tell us what is the best thing for us to do according to His purpose. If we set ourselves up as a judge of them, and say they do not know the best thing for us while we do know, we are saying that God does not know what He is doing, that He does not know how to run our life, that He does not know the best thing for us to do. Failure to submit our judgement is a failure of pride. Therefore, from a point of view of humility, we have an obligation to practice the virtue of obedience.

It has been pointed out previously that there is no better way to manifest charity or the love of God than through obedience. If love of God means union of wills with God, what greater way to manifest union of our will with His than to practice obedience? The virtue of obedience not only unites our will with His, but it unites our intellect and our judgement with His as well. It is, then, actually the beginning of eternal life on earth. For the essence of heaven will be having our intellect completely united with the mind of God and our will completely united with His will. We shall know infinite truth as it is, and love it as it is. Obedience is the beginning of that life on earth. It is to live the life of heaven now, united with God by having our minds and wills united to His mind and will.

Spirit of Obedience Comes Only with Effort

Someone once very mistakenly remarked that acquiring the spirit of obedience was the work of a lifetime. True, it is a lifetime's work if we imagine it will be handed to us on a tray. On our death-bed, we shall discover that we are still waiting for the tray to be brought in, unless we do something about it ourselves. It is a struggle, but if we are to succeed, we have to be motivated, first of all, to *want* to struggle. Perhaps the strongest motive for striving to develop the spirit of obedience is this: If we do not have it to some degree, we might as well forget the religious life and forget community life, for according to Saint Thomas, the essence of religious life is obedience.

We came to the community to seek perfection. Among the means the community offers us is the opportunity to be told at every minute of our day what God wants of us and what His will is for us; it gives us the chance to be moved like a pawn on a chess board by God Himself through human beings. Thus, we need have no concern, no worry to find out *what* God wants of us at any moment of our life in religion. Our only concern is to do what He wants in the best way we can to please Him. We don't have to wonder what we should do. He tells us every minute of the day. We have but to do it the best way we can, whether it be sweeping, or sewing, or nursing, or teaching, or studying, or keeping books, or whatever. Unless we do that, we are not Religious at heart, we are not living the religious life, no matter how well we look in the habit.

For a Religious to say it is a lifetime's work to acquire the spirit of obedience is like a student at a music school saying, "It is a lifetime's work to learn to play a violin. I'll probably die and never know how to play it." He will if he expects to sit around and learn to play the violin automatically, or by listening to recordings of violin playing. So, too, we, as Religious, have to get down to practice the virtue of obedience day after day if we are to acquire a facility in it. To be sure, it is work, and hard work; but it is the work we came to do. The essence of religious life is obedience, so we dare not sit back resting and say, "My, it's hard to do." This is what we should be working at.

Religious Life Means Giving Self to God

The purpose of our training in the novitiate was to teach us that we live religious life only to give ourselves to God, to have Him move us as He will, to be a tool in His hands like a file or chisel in the hands of an artisan. If we resist His every movement, how is God going to reproduce His likeness in our soul? If He pushes the chisel one way and we slide off the other, which is what we do when we set our mind and judgement against the orders of superiors, how can He carve His likeness in us? If we thought we could run our lives so well, why did we voluntarily give ourselves into the hands of God to be run through His representatives? If giving ourselves to God means anything, it means letting Him run our lives.

The truth of the matter is we came to religious life to give ourselves to God, to be moved by Him; and if we have not been trying to form the habit of being submissive in mind and will to Him, we are wasting our time because, as has been said, that is the essence of religious life and the cause of the glory it gives to God. That submission of will and judgement, that devotion of our faculties to the service of God for which they were made is what makes the whole of our life an act of religion, an act of worship of God.

On the contrary, if we ourselves are deciding what to do, and failing to submit our judgement, we are devoting our faculties to the service of ourselves; we are loving ourselves and not God.

Therefore, the statement that it is a lifetime's work to acquire the spirit of obedience must be condemned. That spirit is not a pleasing bit of decoration on the religious life. It is its essence. For example, if someone were a teacher of English, it would be very helpful to him to know Latin, just as it would be a good thing for a teacher of Spanish to be able to speak French. But while it would be beneficial, it is *not essential* for either teacher to know the other language.

But the *fitness* of an English teacher knowing Latin is vastly different from the *necessity* of a professional water polo player knowing how to swim. Knowing how to swim for a water polo player is not only desirable; it is absolutely essential. If he does not know how to swim, he will sink, and moreover probably drown. Therefore, it is essential that he know how to swim.

Similarly, to suggest that it is a lifetime's work for a Religious to acquire the spirit of obedience, that is, to acquire a habit of submitting will and judgement, is just as ridiculous as to say it is a lifetime's work for a water polo player to learn to swim, or that it is a lifetime's work for a professional hockey player to learn how to skate. If the one does not know how to swim, he can not be a water polo player at all; if the other does not know how to skate, he can not be a professional hockey player at all. The same is true of religious life. If we do not have the spirit of obedience very soon after its inception, we will sink in as far as living it fruitfully is concerned. The spirit of obedience and submission of judgement is not merely something pleasant to have, or that we can take our time and work at slowly for the rest of our lives. It is absolutely essential for living the religious life.

Spirit of Obedience Must Be Developed Early

Our novitiate is the practice period, the time when we are thrown into the pool, so to speak, like the beginning water polo player, to learn how to flail our arms about in order to stay above water. But we will never be a real water polo player until we have developed the ability to swim. So, too, we will never be true religious or true members of any religious community, until we have learned to submit our will and judgement, or, in other words, until we have the spirit of obedience.

The sooner we learn to swim, the sooner we shall be able to concentrate on playing water polo itself; and the sooner we learn to have the spirit of obedience, the sooner we can concentrate on living our religious life and being good Religious.

What we must be busy at from the very beginning is developing the spirit of obedience. This is not a question of choice. This is our Father's business which we must be about constantly. God is ever pouring down His grace on us to help us achieve this end. It will not be wanting ever. He has called us to the spirit of obedience in the religious life. "Unto this, indeed, you have been called." "For I have given you an example, that as I have done to you, so you also should do." The Son of God was obedient to fallible, ignorant, evil men. "Thou wouldst have no power at all over me were it not given thee from above," He said to sensual, proud Pilate. "You would have no power over me." But He admits that Pilate, the pagan prince, did have power from heaven over Him who was God himself, who had created Pilate out of nothing. Moreover, when Pilate said, "Take him you and crucify him," Christ submitted His will and His judgement to Pilate's betrayal of Him. From a human standpoint, His crucifixion was not wise, nor the best thing. But Christ judged what was best for Him because the Father willed it, and through it we and all of mankind were redeemed. If He had not submitted His judgement, if He had died rebelling, we would not have been saved. So Christ has asked us to do nothing He has not first done Himself. He has done us the honor of calling us to follow Him in that same path of obedience, of submission of our will and judgement to that of our Father in heaven.

CHAPTER VIII

How To Be Obedient

IN VIEW OF THE SPLENDOR and importance of the virtue of
obedience it is imperative to discover means that will
help us acquire this virtue and its spirit. First of all in
this quest, we are aware that what is most likely to be
lacking in our obedience is the proper motive. There the
vitiating wrong motives, like termites, are calculated to
perpetrate their devastating work. We are so prone to judge
by our feelings or reason whether a command does or does
not seem right to us, whether it seems sensible or not. We
are so likely to do what we ought according as our mood
is one of not being too tired, or feeling like it, or because
we like it, or for any of those motives which destroy the
virtue of obedience. We so often act only from a motive
of enlightened self-interest or sensuality.

Therefore, it is necessary to strive to purify our motives.
When we are tempted to act from some wrong or unworthy motive, we should strive to act contrary to the temptation and purify our motive. We can not help being
tempted. Actually, overcoming temptation is one of the
ways in which we reproduce the likeness of Christ in ourselves, one of the ways we earn heaven. But we can help

140

succumbing to the temptation. God gives His grace for that purpose. We can, with His help, overcome the temptation and make it an occasion of an act of virtue by purifying our motive.

Necessity of the Spirit of Faith

Again, if we love God and want to show Him that we love Him in the practice of the virtue of obedience, we shall develop our spirit of *faith*, faith to see Him in our superiors as well as in our rules and in all the external circumstances of obedience.

If a companion comes to tell us we are wanted on the phone for a long distance call, we go to the phone. We are excited, and our heart is beating at what is going to happen. It makes no difference to us whether the phone is black or gray or blue; whether there are finger marks on it, whether it was lying on the table, or somebody handed it to us; all we are interested in is the voice that is going to come through it into our ear and the message it will convey. We prescind entirely from the instrument; whether it is old fashioned, or whether it is new. Why? Because we are listening for the voice of a loved one coming through it.

So, too, if we have the spirit of faith, we listen for the voice of God coming through God's instrument, which may be the superior, or the book of rules, or customs. If we have the spirit of faith, we shall prescind from the person of the superior altogether. We shall not think of her virtues, or her qualifications, whether she reprimanded us or gave us an ice cream cone ten minutes ago. Just as we are concerned not with the nature of the instrument but only the message transmitted through the phone, so we are anxious only to hear God's message transmitted to us through the human instrument which He uses. Therefore we must develop a spirit of faith, of seeing or hearing God speaking to us through our superiors.

Necessity of the Spirit of Charity

Furthermore, the spirit of obedience can perdure only if it is founded on a spirit of *charity*. We have to be willing habitually to overlook defects, not fixing our attention on the flaws we think we see in superiors. We must develop the right attitude toward the ones God has chosen to manifest His will to us, the ones who give us His commands. Above all, developing the spirit of obedience will necessitate our inexorable fighting of anything like an antipathy towards our superior. It is perfectly conceivable that such antipathies might arise; the devil may put them into our heart. But we must struggle against human nature; if we do not, the practice of obedience becomes increasingly difficult.

Besides developing a proper attitude toward our superior, an additional means is to develop a right attitude toward the commands we receive. We must strive habitually to see the directions of superiors through the eyes of faith. This means we do not judge them critically, with prejudice and passion, but only by faith. We must strive to see them clearly and purely as a manifestation of God's will for us, and to say to ourselves as we hear them: "I don't know why, and I don't care why; this I know: This order is what God wants."

Consequently, we have to fight unceasingly against giving in to moodiness and resentment at what we are told to do. We must refrain from entertaining human reasons why we do not want to do what we are told, or why we do not feel like doing it, and, as a result, indulging in criticism and murmuring about what superiors tell us to do, for criticism and murmuring sound the death knell of the spirit of obedience.

The Termites of Obedience

Furthermore, we should not permit ourselves to dwell on any apparent imprudence or un-wisdom we might be tempted to see in any order or thing we are told to do. In obedience, there can be no question of deciding before we act whether a command is right, whether it seems right to us, whether it seems good to us, whether it seems reasonable to us, whether it seems profitable to us, whether it seems comfortable to us, whether it seems advantageous to us. None of these considerations has anything constructive to do with the virtue of obedience any more than termites have any thing constructive to do with a house. Actually, the relationship between termites and the foundation of the house is one of destruction. Termites are the enemies, the destroyers of the house's support.

So, also, judging whether a thing we are told to do is right to us, whether it is proper, fitting, advantageous, sensible, prudent, wise, or convenient has a relationship of destruction to the supernatural virtue of obedience. Such questions are the termites that destroy the virtue of obedience. Once we make the carrying out of a command contingent upon our knowing why, we have destroyed supernatural obedience. Such questions as: "Why do I have to do this?" destroy the virtue of obedience because obviously in such a case, we are not obeying for the reason that God commands us but because what we are told to do seems right to us.

All the trouble in the world started with the question: "why?" The serpent said to Eve, "Why has God commanded you not to eat of this fruit?" Eve said to herself, "Yes, I wonder why? Why did He say that?" Then the devil began to suggest the reasons why: "Because you will be as smart as He is if you do." The obedient course would have been for her to accept God's will. But she began to speculate and look for reasons in her own puny mind why He had forbidden her to touch that fruit. "Why did He forbid me? Why doesn't He let me eat it? Why can't I? Why do I have to eat this fruit instead of that? I wonder why He told me that? It seems foolish to tell me I can't eat that one fruit. If I can eat everything else, why shouldn't I be able to eat that? It looks just like all the others."

So often we reason and speculate with ourselves in this same way: "Why did they tell me to do this? What is the sense of having a rule about that? Why do we have that foolish custom? I am not going to do that. It doesn't seem sensible to me. It doesn't seem right to me. Why?" As has been said, in asking such questions, we destroy the virtue of obedience. There can be no virtue of obedience exercised then because the motive for the supernatural virtue of obedience is clearly lacking. If we do keep any commands in such circumstances, we do so because it seems right to us, or reasonable to us, or for some other such reason, but certainly not because our infinitely wise Father is telling us.

Obedience and Selfish Pride

Not carrying out such commands is not necessarily the formal sin of disobedience, unless we fail to carry them out simply out of contempt, unless we disobey simply because we are commanded. But for the most part, such an attitude would more properly indicate a sin of pride. We say, in effect, to ourself: "They are not going to tell me what to do. Haven't they heard about me? I'll make a few photostats of my record and pass them around and let these people know whom they are telling to do these things. That was all right fifty or a hundred years ago when the community was founded. But this is the twentieth century." So, while the described attitude might not be a sin of disobedience, it could certainly be a sin against faith, or of imprudence; it could be a sin of intellectual pride.

When we ask why, we are pitting our judgement against that of God's representatives who are, as it were, standing up on a tower like lifeguards on a beach, looking over the whole shore. They see much more than we see from our lowly position on the ground. They have greater sources of knowledge, first of all by virtue of the grace of their state. They see things we do not have the grace to see. Furthermore, by virtue of the information they have at their disposal, they know things we can not know because God has not made the facts available to us. They are in a better position to judge of the wisdom of what they tell us to do than we.

Furthermore, the function of the superior is to care for the *common good,* the good of all. Authority exists for that reason, and very often the common good demands something that, to a selfish individual, may not go down so well. It may not be objectively the best thing for an individual considered in herself, as though she were the only person in the world. But the superior knows the needs of all. Therefore, with our selfish mind, we might often judge that our task is foolish when it is not so at all. For example, we might own our own home and the best thing for us would be to continue living in it. But the governor of the state might say: "I am sorry; we have to destroy your house in order to build a road where it stands." Obviously, it is not the best arrangement for us, but it is the best thing for the common good. However, because we are selfish, we are not concerned with the common good if it is costly to us, and we are inclined to reject its claims.

Whenever we question the wisdom of what we are told to do, if we were honest, we would admit that were we judging objectively, we would most likely conclude that it would not be so unwise if someone else were told to do what we have been told to do. "Don't let them tell me to do it," we say to ourselves, "because it is foolish. But it is all right for someone else." We make decisions like that because our judgements concerning ourselves are clouded by prejudice and passion and pride and selfishness and self-seeking, by concern for our own comfort and our own pleasure.

Obedience and Humility

A good remedy for such failure is *humility* in the maintaining of our own opinion and judgement. Humility is the best and the greatest guardian of the virtue of obedience, particularly insofar as it demands submission of our judgement. We should develop the habit of not examining critically the orders given to us by superiors or rule. We should strive to develop a habit of not thinking of them objectively, but recalling only that we have heard a message from God; therefore we must go and do it.

It is perfectly understandable that we be tempted not to submit our judgement, not only to the superior, but even to the rules. There is nothing so sacred about the Holy Rules that we cannot be tempted against them. If we can be tempted by the devil or nature against the very commandments of God, for a greater reason we can be tempted against the rules of our community.

But we cannot set ourselves up as a tribunal judging God and His decrees, saying: "I can't see why that commandment, 'Thou shalt not steal' should apply to me. It is a contradiction to my mind. If I need what another has, why can't I go and get it?" Moreover, we do not submit our judgement to God's will if we say, "I'll do it because God commands it; but I still think it is a stupid commandment. If I want to steal, then it is all right for me to steal." We can be tempted to set up our own "do-it-yourself" court of appeals and reason in the same way about the prescripts of our rule or orders of our superiors.

If we have a habit of doing so, how can we overcome this practice of running every order we receive through the IBM machine of our mind to find out whether it coincides perfectly with what we, in the conceits of our own wisdom, judge to be the right thing to do? As was mentioned earlier, the way to conquer a vice is to develop the opposite virtue.

Therefore, we must think about it at our morning meditation, and resolve to pray on the very first occasion we are tempted to judge whether something we are commanded is objectively the best thing or not to do. Is it likely to be right after breakfast, when assignments are given? Will it possibly be at a certain time in our duty? Will it be when the worklist is posted? Whenever today we are tempted to think: "Why are they telling me to do that?" we resolve to say such and such a prayer over and over again, to ask God to let us think only of His will, and for strength to do what we are asked only because it is His will. We resolve to say that prayer over and over again, until the temptation is gone. Then, at noon examen, we discover whether we kept our resolution or not. If we did, we thank God; if we didn't, we express sorrow. In either case, we renew our resolution for the afternoon, trying to foresee the occasion that might arise in the afternoon when we shall be tempted not to submit our judgement.

Seeking to Discover What God Wants

Another practical means of acquiring a facility in the virtue of obedience is to develop the habit of deliberately *seeking to discover* God's will in every instance we possibly can, but particularly in those instances in which we might be tempted to exercise our liberty *without* determining God's will. For example, suppose we are planning to do a certain thing we would like to do. We reason to ourself: "I don't see why the superior would object to my doing it. Other people have done it, so I might as well go ahead and do it without bothering to ask her." Thinking such thoughts, we are concentrating on doing our own will. On the other hand, if we ask about it, God's will is definitely signified in regard to that act. We thereby get the merit of the virtue of obedience if we have the intention of carrying out God's will in doing it. The more we are able to find out the wishes of a superior in every instance, the more we make it possible for the virtue of obedience to influence every moment of our lives, for the wishes of the superior are God's will in our regard.

If we never have to give an account to God of what we do from the virtue of obedience, it is a very valuable tool with which to work at all times. Sensibly then, we should not let it rust out but use it constantly by striving to bring as much of our life as possible under the influence of this virtue, trying to discover God's will, as often and as clearly as we can. We thereby increase our merit tremendously, for we thus use our will, the greatest faculty God has given us, for the greatest purpose possible, namely, submitting it to God and His will.

Sincerity in the Search for God's Will

But we must be *sincere* in seeking to discover God's will, not just pretending. It is easy to deceive ourself here. Suppose, for example, we decide we would like to make a feast day gift for somebody. We have all the materials salvaged from last Christmas. We say to ourself, "I think I'll go and ask permission anyway. I know Sister will approve; it is a fine idea." So we go and say, "Sister, I would like to make a feast day gift for X. I have all the material I've saved since last Christmas." Sister answers, "No, I think you had better not do that; it is not customary." "All right, thank you, Sister," we say as we come out dejectedly and start to talk to ourself: "I've saved all this miserable stuff since last Christmas; now, why won't she let me use it to make this gift? I'll go ahead and make it anyway, and maybe she will change her mind. She just doesn't like X."

Such thinking and mumbling to ourself is an indication that while we went in ostensibly to find out the wishes of the superior, and consequently the will of God, we were not really trying to find it out at all. Actually, we were trying to get the superior to wish what we wished. We made a nodding bow to convention. Permission should have been asked and we asked it. But the virtue of obedience is in the mind and heart, and while we went through the formality of asking permission, our conduct indicated that we did not want to find out what God wanted at all.

Therefore, when we ask permissions to find out God's will, we should seek it with indifference. We should purify our intention before we ask any permission, saying to ourselves: "I am going to the office to ask this permission; but whatever You want, dear Lord, is what I want. My reason for going is to find out whether You want me to have it or not. If You say yes, all right; if You say no, all right." We have then made the offering of our joy or disappointments. We have purified our intention from the very beginning.

True, when we are refused a permission, feelings might well up in us; but they will not vitiate our intention or our act of virtue, provided we don't give in to them, provided we combat them. Therefore, if we would have the virtue of obedience, we should strive to purify our motives, our intention before our asking permissions.

Again, in asking permissions, we must avoid any kind of *deceit* of lack of simplicity to get our own way. Sometimes we can ask a permission but we know full well we are not really trying to find out God's will at all. We know from the way we seek the permissions. If we were honest, we would have to admit that our purpose in asking permission is not to find out God's will or what the superior wants, but to cajole the superior into wanting what we want, or to make it so uncomfortable for the superior, to so wring her heart, that she has to give us what we want. Such procedure is not practicing the virtue of obedience. It is not seeking to find out God's will. If we have the true spirit of obedience, we frankly do try to discover God's will without trickery or deceit, without scheming to get our own will.

Submission of Judgement and Representation

In the practice of the virtue of obedience problems sometimes arise in regard to the element of *judgement*. It has been said that submission of the judgement means we look upon orders we receive through the eyes of faith. We admit to ourselves that what we are told is best for us at this particular moment because it is God's will for us. He is telling us to do it through a superior, who is His human instrument. But the fact that His instrument is human means that it is subject to error. However, even if we suspect the superior is wrong in what she tells us to do, we are not wrong in doing it. Because the superior told us to do it, we will not have to account to God for doing it, but we are accountable for the way we do it.

But suppose the superior tells us to do something and we have good reason to suspect that in telling us, she did not know or has forgotten some important circumstance. Suppose she says, "Sisters, you are to go for a walk this afternoon at five o'clock." In telling us that, it is obvious that the superior has completely forgotten that she posted a notice of a conference to be given at five o'clock. Perfect obedience and submission of judgement does not constrain us to say to ourself, "Sister said for us to go for a walk; therefore, we will go for a walk." Charity demands that the superior not be put on the spot by having the whole community out in the garden when all were supposed to be in the chapel. Charity, or in some cases justice, would constrain us to say to her, "Sister, I was wondering if you forgot that there was going to be a conference." In a spirit of humility and charity we represent the circumstance we think the superior is not aware of or has forgotten.

When Representation Should Be Made

But it is important to be able to discern precisely when we should represent. We should do this when we think we possess some fact or piece of knowledge which superiors did not have or did not advert to when they gave the command, and which fact might alter their decision or command. If we have a reasonable doubt, it is better to be safe than to be sorry, and make the representation. We never do any harm by representing, provided we represent in a spirit of humility and charity. It is understood of course that such representation refers only to orders received from superiors. It would be very imprudent to go to a superior and say, "Sister, I think there was something Holy Founder was not aware of when he wrote this rule."

It is likewise important that we understand the relationship between representation and obedience of the judgement, or judging that what we are told to do is the best thing for us here and now. We should represent only when it would appear that the superior did not know some factor that we know, which might influence her command. Having represented that information, we then submit our will and judgement to whatever the superior says *after* she has the information.

A safe rule of thumb is to be cautious about representing when told to do something, if the information or circumstance to be manifested affects only us, or causes us alone hardship. On the other hand, if we are representing information which affects the common good, we can feel safer from illusion in referring to it. In fact, in such a case, we would have a greater obligation to represent.

Suppose, for example, the Provincial Superior should call and say to us, "Sister, we are going to make you a local superior." Perhaps we have no such aspirations; perhaps we fear it. So we decide selfishly to represent, hoping to get out of the assignment. We say, "Mother, you can't possibly do that; you don't know how stupid I am; you don't know how inept I can be, or what a mess I can make of things." Of course she knows! Don't take it so surely that we have been clever enough to conceal our defects over all these years. Such representation is not virtue but cowardice.

Again, we should suspect our motives in representing if, when we are told to do something, we were to say, "Sister, I am sure you do not know that I dislike doing that kind of thing." Such reasons are not encompassed in the notion of justifiable representation. To say to ourself: "The last superior knew I dislike such tasks and she never used to ask me to do them, so I will represent it to this superior," is not representation but attempt at evasion of duty. Valid representation would demand some objective factor that might affect the community, or the work of the community, or even a problem of personal health. But mere personal feelings or preference do not constitute valid ground for representation.

These then, are some means, in addition to prayer, by which we can develop the habit and spirit of the virtue of obedience. Obviously such a spirit will cost us much pain to self-will. But nothing worthwhile was ever accomplished without suffering. "The servant is not above the master" and our Lord suffered much to be obedient for us. In the Epistle to the Hebrews, Saint Paul tells us: "And he, Son though he was, learned obedience from the things that he suffered." Isn't that beautiful! He learned obedience from the things that He suffered; suffering taught Him to be obedient. The epistle goes on, "And when perfected, he became to all who obey him the cause of eternal salvation, called by God a high priest according to the order of Melchisedek." God has revealed to us that, "He, Son though he was, learned obedience from the things that he suffered; and when perfected, he became" the cause of eternal salvation to those who obey Him. What greater reason could we have for the practice of the virtue of obedience. What greater guarantee for salvation than to be obedient, for He became the cause of eternal salvation to those who obey Him.

CHAPTER IX

Abandonment and Our Sanctification

GOD'S DEALING WITH US and God's work of sanctification in us is a two-fold process. First must come the emptying of ourselves of attachment to self-will and of sin, in order that, secondly, we may be filled with the life of God, that God may fill us with Himself. Self-will and God's will * are incompatible. So, in proportion as we empty ourselves of self-will to allow God's life and grace to flow into us, we shall be sanctified. If a child at the beach has a pail full of sand, and wants to fill the pail with water, he must empty out the sand. To the extent that he takes out sand, he can replace it with water. So, too, to the extent that we empty ourself of the sand of self-will, we can be filled with the life-giving waters of God's grace. Sometimes the taking out of the sand is a long and tedious process, picking out, as it were, one grain of sand at a time with tweezers. That is so when we are taking out the sand ourselves.

But God is also a partner in this emptying process. Whether we ask Him or not, He is vitally interested in our

---

* For a discussion of charity, the companion virtue to obedience in doing what God wants, the reader is referred to the very detailed treatment in KEYS TO THE THIRD FLOOR, in the chapters entitled Love of the Poor, and Love of Enemies.

emptying of ourself and is constantly furnishing the means whereby this may be accomplished. The means He furnishes are the creatures and circumstances about us and the contacts we have with them. He is constantly coming to us, to work in us through the action of His creatures on us and through our contact with creatures. We seldom think of all the endurings and events to which we are subject at every moment of life as God's action on us; yet, in overlooking this fact, we miss their most significant and most valuable aspect.

Each year we prepare for the coming of the Holy Spirit into our souls at Pentecost in order that He may fill us with grace and with life. The Holy Ghost comes to us on Pentecost, as at any other time, to the extent that and in proportion as we have made room for Him; in the degree that we have emptied ourselves of self and self-will, He comes to sanctify us, because He is the sanctifier.

But the Holy Spirit comes to us not only at Pentecost. He constantly comes to us, to act in us, to sanctify us. Otherwise we would not be sanctified. But He comes in a *particular way* on Pentecost because then we commemorate and re-live His first coming. In view of that, we prepare ourselves in a particular way to receive Him. We prepare ourselves to let Him operate in a special way in us.

The Holy Spirit Comes Invisibly and Visibly

But whether on Pentecost Sunday or at any other time, He comes into us in the same *way* as He came to the apostles. He comes in an invisible way, and He comes in a visible way. He came, as we know, to the apostles in an invisible way through the infusion of sanctifying grace and a greater intensification of the divine indwelling. He came also in a visible way, through the creature, *fire*, tongues of fire, suspended over the heads of the apostles.

So, too, He comes to us, first of all, in an invisible way, through the infusion of new grace and greater intensification of the divine indwelling in us. He likewise comes in a visible way, not through the creature, *fire*, as to the apostles, but through *every other creature* with whom and with which we come in contact.

This is a fact which we customarily ignore. We like to think of the Holy Spirit coming to us and of God working in us in His *invisible way*. That is, we like to think of His coming through the infusion of grace, through His strengthening of our soul and invigorating us, that we might be transformed and sanctified in a *painless* way, while we sleep, as it were, through the operation of the Holy Ghost. We like to think about and concentrate on this manner of God's coming.

But we forget about God's *visible* coming to us and God's visible visitation of us through the creatures with whom we come in contact. We forget that every single thing and person, animate and inanimate, which touches upon or affects us in *any* way is God's instrument through which He is operating in us and sanctifying us, especially by giving us an opportunity to empty self of self-will.

Every Creature Is God's Instrument

If all of creation and all creatures are instruments or means which Almighty God has given us to grope our faltering way to Him, then for a greater reason *everything*, every creature is an instrument through which God carries out His work of sanctification in us. God uses *everything* as a means to sanctify us and to bring us to Him.

That is why Saint Paul tells us that to those who love God, "All things work together unto good." *All things!* He excludes nothing, the good, the bad, or the indifferent. If we would know the extent to which all things work together unto good, we have but to recall our Divine Lord telling us that "Not a hair of your head shall perish" without His knowledge and without His permission. The falling of a hair is not, certainly, an important event; and yet, even that, insignificant as it is, is a concern of God's care. So concerned is God with a falling human hair, that He took the trouble, so to speak, to reveal it to mankind, to make it a part of the deposit of faith, a part of that body of truth which God revealed to man in an extraordinary way and preserved for all eternity in the written record of His revelation. So finely does God calculate and take into consideration all things in regard to us that even "the very hairs of our head," He tells us, "are numbered."

Thus, He never ceases coming to us; He never ceases acting in us at every moment of our lives, not only invisibly through His grace, but visibly through the action of creatures with which we come in contact and which come in contact with us. Furthermore, in all this coming into us and in all this operating in us, God, has a *purpose*. His purpose is that He may make us more like Him; that He may give us an opportunity to unite our will to His, thus emptying us of another grain of sand of self-will, and becoming more sanctified still. His purpose is that by our uniting our will to His we may thus glorify Him, and, as a result of that, achieve a greater share of His happiness which He wills for us for all eternity. That is God's *general* purpose and plan for us in all the events and circumstances of our life.

To achieve this master plan, this ultimate objective that He has for us, God directs every *particular* and *individual* event of our lives however insignificant it might seem. God's general overall plan for us links together all the infinitesimally small events and happenings of our lives into what He now sees, and we shall one day see, as an intelligible and intelligent whole.

God Sanctifies Us by Creatures

In every moment of our life, from the time we wake up until we go to bed at night, God is working out His plan in us. He is laying, at every instant, the particular stone that He knows is needed according to the condition of the structure of our individual life, that is demanded by His master plan in order that He may build up in us the likeness of Himself.

In somewhat the same way as a stone mason will sort over and pick out just the correct stone which has the right size, the right shape, the right hue and color, the right texture to fit into the pattern that he is working out in a building, so God does with us. He is the stone mason; we are the building. He picks out the stone that, at any given moment, may be needed to enlighten our mind, or may be needed to strengthen our will, or to purify our senses in order to achieve His purpose. In our judgement, it may have the strangest kind of shape, and color and texture. It may seem the most mis-shapen, mis-fitted stone in the world for Him to lay in the structure of our life at the particular moment; but He knows the need of it. He knows the condition of the structure of our life, the state of our spiritual welfare. He knows what is needed, and what must be done, and what can be done. What must be done, He is doing at every moment of our life, all the while yearning to complete His work, to see the fulness of His operations in us.

So, He comes to us and He acts in us in every single one of the events of our life in order to accomplish His purpose. But our likeness to Him is increased in us only to the extent that we are docile to His operation; it is decreased in us to the extent that we hinder His operation by resistance. He comes and He works in us and operates in us, not as we think He should, or as we would like Him to, but as He knows is best. He comes at every moment, operates in us at every moment through all the creatures with whom we come in contact. He does this, and let it be repeated, to help us to empty ourself of self-will, and of sin, and of attachment to sin, so that we may, in turn, be filled with Him, that we may be filled with His life, that we may be sanctified.

To accomplish this work of our sanctification, He uses the instruments that are at hand, namely, all of the creatures, animate and inanimate, with which we come in contact, and which touch us. Actually, there is an almost infinite number and variety of creatures with whom and with which we come into contact, almost an infinite variety of ways in which they can touch upon us. But God's purpose in it all is to empty us of self and fill us with Him.

If our contacts with creatures affect us adversely, we call it suffering and here is the chief area of our resistance to God's operation in us. But God intends even suffering to detach us from ourselves and to attach us to Him. However, He is able to accomplish His intended work in us through our suffering from contact with creatures, only insofar as we submit to His operation upon us, only insofar as we are docile to His action within us by what He sends us.

If our loving Father is to achieve his purpose, we must submit to His action without reserve, without anxiety and curiosity and murmuring, like a trusting child. But so often we are like spoiled children. We pray (sincerely, we think) for God to make us holy. We ask it everyday in the Mass. Then God takes us at our word. He begins to work in us in the *best* way possible at the moment for His purpose. He starts to work in us through the contact of some creature with us. It may be a disagreeable duty, it may be a change of mission, it may be a contradiction, a provocation by one toward whom we have an aversion; it may be a headache or other physical indisposition; it may be a regulation by the superior; it may be an interference with our plans; it may be a refusal of a permission or a misunderstanding; it may be anything that we do not like, great or small.

But at the first slight contact with the creature which is God's instrument for sanctifying us, we begin to scream and kick and yell. We say, "No! No! not that! Don't work in me in that way! Why does this have to happen to me? What did I do to deserve this? Why do things have to be this way? Why do they have to act like that? Why does she have to do or say that?" In such manner we go on and on like pouting, immature offspring complaining and rebelling against God's wisdom and goodness. Thus, we persist in proving the insincerity of our prayers to God that He take us into His hands to make us holy.

We are not and cannot be sincere in our desires or prayers to be perfect or to be holy unless we refuse to make peace with a habit of complaining and murmuring against God's will; unless we are willing to develop a habit of recognizing His working in us through creatures; unless we work to acquire a facility in trustfully submitting without rebellion and without resentment to the action of our loving Father on us, His children.

This submission, of course, is not to the unpleasant *thing*, the evil that we bear, but our submission is to the *action of God* which is taking place. We submit to the *Will of God* which is bringing about this suffering or this pain which we call evil.

Now, when we mention the will of God and evil in the same breath, we are dealing with a topic which is a scandal and a stumbling block to many, even among the so-called good and learned. Yet Catholic theology teaches that nothing happens in this world unless God expressly wills it, with the exception of sin. As St. Augustine says: "Nothing happens unless the Omnipotent One wills it to happen, either by permitting it to be or by doing it Himself" (P.L., XL, 276—quoted in Tanquerey, *Theol. Dog.*, vol. 2, p. 294). God is the universal cause, the first cause of everything that happens in the world, except sin. No fate or fortune or chance or accident can either smile on us or frown on us to bring us good or to bring us bad. We read in the book of Ecclesiasticus that, "*Good* things and *evil,* life and death, poverty and riches, are from God." Here we have the inspired word of God telling us that both good things and evil are from God. But how can evil be said to be from God?

God's Will and Physical Evil

Before we can answer this question, we must make a distinction. There are two classes of things that we are accustomed to call evil, from our point of view. The first class of things is what we might term physical evils or natural evils such as hunger, sorrow, storms, suffering that arises from earthquakes and floods and fires, illness, death, and things of this nature. They are called evil by us because we do not like them and we do not like to suffer their consequences.

But the fact is that they are not real evils in the sight of God. They are more properly called the fruits of sin and bitter medicines administered by the Divine Physician of souls. These things are evil only from our point of view. They all have positive reality and being. Therefore, they were all necessarily created by Almighty God and received their being from Him and therefore they are good, because everything that God created is good.

Of course, from the very beginning, God's will of good pleasure was that man should *not suffer.* When He created man, He gave him immunity from suffering, immunity from sickness, immunity from death, immunity from ignorance and concupiscence and temptation to sin. He willed that man should not suffer these things; but He willed it *conditionally.* The condition was that man not sin, that man obey His law, that man live up to his part of the agreement with God. But when man failed to observe this condition, then God's will manifested itself in His willing the consequences of sin to come upon men in order to achieve His purpose in creation. Therefore, ultimately, all suffering, all pain, all sorrow, all misunderstanding, all disorder is traceable to sin. It is willed by God now *per accidens;* that is, God wills the natural and physical evil, but for the greater good He brings about through it. But it was not so from the beginning. His will originally was that we should be preserved from all these calamities on condition that we did His will. Man did not, and hence God wills the natural consequences of sin upon men.

For example, we think of cancer as being evil. But cancer is a reality that was created by Almighty God for a purpose and it is good. A good cancer is a cancer that does what it is supposed to do, i.e., kill somebody. We think of it as evil because it makes us or our loved ones suffer; but God made cancer to work out His Providence among men, even though, had man not sinned, He would not have willed man to suffer from cancer; He does so now only for the good of the universe. How many souls have returned to God and saved their souls because they were thus stricken? How many have become saints from the patient endurance of the sufferings of cancer? It is an instrument of God's justice, His mercy, and His love. Again, we call a storm or a hurricane evil; but God created it and therefore it is good. A good hurricane is one that blows things down, for that is what God made it to do; although, again, He wills it thus *per accidens* in order to bring about a greater good. All such things are evil only from our point of view. These physical things that we call evils, evils of nature, are not evil in themselves. All of them God wills. He creates them; He brings them into being for His own good purposes. They could not exist without or apart from the will of God.

God's Will and Moral Evil

But in addition to the physical consequences of sin which we call evil, there is a second class of evil, the only real evil, which is moral evil or sin itself. Now, what is the relation of sin to the will of God? Here again we must make a distinction. In every sin, we can distinguish two aspects. First of all, there is the *guilt* of sin or the evil will or intention in the sinner. Secondly there are the effects of that sin or what the theologians call the punishment of sin.

The effects of the sin are seen in the sinner himself and in all those who suffer from his sin. For example, there are the humiliations, the discomfort, the injury that we suffer from somebody else's sin, because somebody slanders us, or maligns us, or because somebody does us an injustice or an injury. Now, God does not will positively the *guilt* of sin in that person. That is contrary to God's goodness. But, *per accidens*, and to work out His plan in the world and thus achieve the ultimate good, God does will the *effects* of that man's sin, both on the sinner himself and on us who suffer from the man's sin. These effects of sin are not moral evil and unless God willed them, in some way, they could not happen. They are, again, physical evil, as we term it, or natural evil. So, if we set aside in our mind, or prescind from or except the actual guilt of sin in a man's will, all of the effects of sin, all of the punishment which we suffer from our own or the sin of another are caused ultimately by God; they are willed by God; and they are pleasing to God for they are working out His Providence in this world which is as it is because of sin.

God's Permissive Will

But while God wills the punishment of sin, he only *permits* the evil will or the guilt of sin to exist. For example, suppose a man were to throw a hand grenade over the wall of a school yard and kill nearly a hundred children and then flee in a stolen car. All of those acts which the man did, God willed, or he could not have done them. He could not lift the grenade to pull out the firing pin with his teeth unless God gave him the strength. It is the same motion that God gives him strength to perform when he lifts food to his mouth on a fork. He could not move his legs to run to the stolen car unless God gave him the strength, for that is the same motion that God would give him to walk to church on Sunday. He could not reach out his hand to start the motor unless God gave him the strength, just as surely as a bee can not buzz his wings unless God wills it, as truly as a mosquito can not bite unless God wills it. Those physical actions which the man performed were not evil in themselves. It is not evil to pull a firing pin with the teeth. It is not evil to throw an object.

The evil was in the man's will, and that evil was from him and not from God. It was a lack of good that should have been in the man's will, just as darkness is a lack of light. Ever since God said, "Let there be light," the only way to produce darkness is to shut out that light. So, too, the only way to produce evil is to shut out the good that should be in the human will. So, then, we must say that God permitted the evil will of the grenade thrower, but He willed, *per accidens,* the effects on the children and on the school yard, effects which we call evil, but which really are not evil in the sight of God because through them He works out His purposes for His honor and glory and the greater good of men.

Perhaps an example will clarify how the man's will is the cause of evil in the man's action, which God wills. Suppose we have a blister on our heel. We can walk, but we walk with a limp. It is painful; it is awkward to walk. But what is the cause of that limp? Is it our *soul* or life principle which gives motion to our foot and enables us to walk, and without which we could not walk? No, our soul applies the motion to the foot in the same way it did when the foot was healthy. It is the blister that causes us to limp. The blister is an obstacle that stands in the way of the motion which our soul imparts to our foot. So, too, God is the first cause and the power behind every action that a sinner does. What is the cause of the evil in the action? The blister, that is, the man's own bad will which interferes with God's motion and stands between it and the effect He would produce.

So, we can say that sin, the only real evil, is from God in this way: He permits the evil will or guilt in a man, but positively *wills, per accidens,* as has been said, all of the effects of sin or punishment of sin. Otherwise they could not possibly exist. Therefore, we should attribute nothing to chance, or to fate, or to the ill will of men. It is wrong to say that something happened because of someone's ill will towards us. "This happened," we say, "because she hates me. This happened because she wanted to hurt me." No. God has arranged it all. God guided the hand that struck us. God moved the tongue that slandered us, and God gave strength to the feet that trampled us. They could not move unless God willed them to move. Almighty God says of Himself, through the Prophet Isaias, "I form the light and create darkness. I made peace and create evil." God said, "I create evil." He creates evil by *permitting* the guilt of sin but positively *willing* the effects of sin, the suffering which comes from sin, again, *per accidens,* in order that He bring about our greater good and His honor and glory.

How God Permits Sin

But it is imperative that we know clearly and precisely what we mean when we say that God permits sin. Does saying that God permits sin mean that God sits idly by doing nothing to prevent evil? Does it mean that He is not interested; that He looks down as an idle spectator while men assail one another, while men fight and quarrel with one another, while men hurt one another, ruin justice, and bring sorrow on one another? No, not at all! Such a conclusion shows a rank misunderstanding of the nature of God's permissive will. Furthermore, this very misunderstanding of the nature of God's permissive will causes untold discontent and unhappiness and misery and a lack of advancement and holiness and in the spiritual life in many. In order to have a true understanding of the nature of God's permissive will, we should always remember that it must be confined to the question of real *evil* as such, the evil of sin, moral evil.

To repeat, the *only* circumstance in which we can speak of God's *permissive* will, or say that He *permits* something is when there is question of moral evil or *sin. Everything else* that we are accustomed to call evil, including the effects of sin, God wills positively even though such would not have been the case had man not sinned. So let us not be apologizing for God. He knows what He does, and He has no need of our apologies when He strikes with apparent evil either ourselves or someone whom we are trying to comfort.

Physical or natural evils which cause disturbance, pain, suffering and death, such as poverty, imprisonment, disease, and illness, humiliation, and so on are not evil in themselves. They are not evil from God's point of view. They are the instruments that He wills to use to empty us of self-will, to correct us, and to give us a chance to merit a higher place in heaven by carrying the cross and being more like Him. They are evil only from our point of view just as bitter medicine is not evil from the mother's point of view but only from the child's. She knows it is a good, calculated to make her child better. The child thinks it is evil, but it is not, really. So too, all the things for which we are accustomed to apologize for God for letting happen by saying He permits them, all these natural physical evils are not really evil. Let us, then, even if no one else will, profess *faith* in God's wisdom and goodness and say the *truth* that God *wills* them for our own greater good!

But our question now is *how* does God permit the evil of sin? Is it with some kind of passive permission such as we might have when we would say, "It is snowing out, so we will let it snow because we can not do anything about it?" Not at all. God does not permit things because He can not do anything about them. He does not permit things as we might be said to permit what we can not prevent or what we would prefer not to have happen. The reason is, first of all, that everything that will be or that will happen in this world, even sin, God forsees. He knows about it and has known for all eternity. Furthermore everything that is, or will be, or that can happen, even sin, God could hinder, God could stop if He so wanted. But since He does not stop or hinder either sin in general, or any particular sin, then He must be said to want it or will it in some way. Thus, from all eternity, Almighty God decreed and willed *to permit* sin. Therefore, God permits sin, not by being unwilling that it happen, but by *willing to permit it*. There is in Almighty God a positive will of permitting the evil of the guilt of sin.

Why God Permits Sin

Why God permits the evil of the guilt of sin must remain ultimately one of the great mysteries of our life. Saint Augustine summed up all the possible reasons for it by saying that He permits the evil or guilt of sin in order that He might draw out of it a greater good than if He had not permitted the sin. This is true even if we can not see the greater good that He brings about. Sometimes we can, but our ability or inability to see the greater good alters not one iota the fact that God does produce greater good from the sin He permits than would be if He did not permit it.

For example, God willed to *permit* the sin of the murder

of His own Divine Son by the deicides of Jerusalem. But He did not permit, but *willed* the nails to go into His hands and feet, the thorns to pierce His brow, and the spear to pierce His side. Those *effects* of sin He *willed;* the guilt of the sin, the evil will in the men's heart he *permitted.* And that permission of sin which Almighty God willed redounded to the good of the whole human race. It showed forth the goodness and the power and the majesty and the love of Almighty God. If God, from all eternity, had not willed to permit that sin of deicide, we would not be able to kneel today in our holy habit in the presence of the Most Blessed Sacrament. We would not be able to read His doctrine in these pages.

Actually, God's drawing good out of evil shows the wonders of His Providence. Anyone can produce good from good, but it is a sign of greatness to draw good from evil. For example, any licensed pilot should be expected to bring in, in good weather, a plane which is in sound condition; but it is a mark of a great pilot to bring in a plane in a raging storm when all the engines but one are out and the landing gear is broken. So, God's drawing good out of evil is a sign or mark of His power and greatness.

Hence it is that, by the wickedness which he permits in some men, He stimulates others to goodness and virtue and sanctity. For example, God willed to *permit* the evil of guilt in Hitler and so many inhuman Nazis and communists who ran the concentration camps during World War II. God willed to *permit* their evil will; but, *per accidens,* He *willed positively* all the suffering and the misery borne by the prisoners in those camps. Because of that suffering, many of them are saints before the throne of God today singing, "Holy, holy, holy, Lord God of hosts," who would not be there had God not permitted the evil will and the sin of their persecutors. But whether we in any way can see what good results might come about, we know that the cause in God for

His permitting the evil of the guilt of sin is that He might draw greater good from it.

Therefore, if we complain about what happens to us from the sin of others, we are complaining about what God wills for our greater good. This complaining marks the difference between the saints and us. They saw God as the doer of everything that happened to them. They disregarded altogether the evil will and sin of the one who offended and injured them, and concentrated only on the thought of the effects in them. Consequently, they saw God's will as the primary actual and efficient cause of everything that happened to them. They were secure in the knowledge that God is so good that He would will and could will nothing to happen to them unless it was for their own greater good.

Those Who Injure Us Do God's Will

Thus, everyone who hurts or injures us by sin acts out a dual role. They play two parts: The first part is that in which they have an evil will, in which they devise an evil plan against us. The second part they play is that in which they have power to and are able to *externalize* their evil plan, to put it into action. In this role, they play the part of instruments of God. They are doing God's work, even though they may be ignorant of it, because, in reality, God is willing for us the effects of those sins. Through those effects, God is working in us to empty us of self, that He might fill us with His grace and His will, in order that He might give us an opportunity to merit a higher place in heaven by bearing the cross as He did.

Thus, we see the folly of complaining about what happens to us, because to do so is to complain against the merciful hand of God. Saint Augustine points it out in this way: If we find fault with those who by sin and by bad intention hurt or injure us, what are we really finding fault with? Are we finding fault with their evil will? Or are we finding fault with their power and ability to put that evil will into action, so that we suffer the effects? Or are we finding fault with both? It is useless, he tells us, to find fault with their evil will, because if they only have an evil will against us, and are powerless to implement it or to put it into action, they can never hurt us. They are like a roaring lion in a cage; he can't get out so he can not hurt us. We can stick out our tongue at him with impunity. So, too, their evil will can't hurt us unless they have power to externalize it, that is, to say that word or to do that thing against us which their evil will is ordering.

But we must not complain about their power to put their evil will into effect, because that power they get from God. It is God working in them. Thus, when we complain about the power they have to perpetrate their evil, we are complaining about God. As Saint Paul says, there is no power but from God. Any tongue, any hands, any lips, any mind that injures us, receives the power to move and to injure us from God. Thus, if it came from God, it is praiseworthy.

Again, we must recall here that God can permit or will nothing that is not for our greater good. God does nothing unjust against us or against anyone. If one man kills another, God permits the guilt of that sin and cooperates in giving the power to do it. True, the man kills the other man unjustly, but God does not permit the sin unjustly. So also, the unjust will of the murderer is to be condemned, but the just permission of God is to be praised, as God is to be praised in all of his works.

The recognition of this fact as has been said, marks the difference between the saints and us. The saints had no thought at all of who injured them; they thought only of God who permitted the injury. That is why they travelled toward sanctity with giant strides. They regarded injuries as blessings. For example, there is not a saint in the long calendar of the history of the Church who practiced this more perfectly, who exemplified it and taught it more in season and out than the glorious Saint Vincent DePaul. Time after time, as we read in his biography, he talks of persecutions, of lawsuits, of discouraging failures in his community works in Madagascar. In every instance, he refers to these calamities as blessings from God. Every misfortune that men might call evil, he regarded as a blessing. He believed in that beatitude of Christ: "Blessed are they who suffer persecution for justice sake."

The Importance of Overcoming Feelings

So, it will be a happy day for us when we are able to rise above merely natural feelings of suffering and sorrow in trials, and perceive and realize *God's* working within us by means of present suffering. The more insensible we become to natural human feelings of suffering and pain, the more we overlook them, the more we become alive to the astounding fact that Almighty God, Our Father, is *stooping*, as it were, at this very instant, to work out His plan in our own soul through this thing that is happening to us. The more we are willing to forget self in our trials, the more we recognize that *Digitus Dei est hic* (the finger of God is here) right in our very own life.

Of course, we shall continue to *feel* these sufferings. No amount of virtue will ever deprive a man of his sense of feeling. But, we shall not dread affliction that comes upon us. Adversity will befall us, it is true, but it will not overcome us because we shall know that it is God's will for us, that it pleases God that we have this adversity, and we must struggle that it please us too.

So, the more we are able to rise above our feelings in our trials, the more we shall be aware that God is stooping to be interested in us, to sanctify us, to bring us to a greater capacity to glorify Him and enjoy His happiness by means of all these creatures with which we come in contact, by means of all these events that transpire in our life. If we could only see *that* and recognize *that*, how fortunate we would be.

But we know from bitter experience that it is difficult to accept sufferings well. Often a slight trouble can cast us down, and a slightly greater trouble can crush us. We are such tender, hothouse flowers that we dread and cringe from every touch of the wind, of the rain, of the sun, of the frost. Our habit of seeking self-satisfaction, of seeking our own pleasures, our own ease, seeking to satisfy our aesthetic tastes and so on, has made us soft, incapable of putting up with anything that is difficult or hard.

Because we resist God's purifying action of suffering so much, His work in us does not bring about the progress that He intends it to bring. Instead, it seems to increase our guilt or our imperfection. We become embittered and impatient with suffering, and we revolt against it. If we do submit, too often it is with murmuring and complaint. But in showing ill will and resentment toward suffering, we are repulsing God and His loving operations in us. We are obstructing the fatherly operations by which He wants to sanctify us.

Therein lies the tragedy of living by our senses; the tragedy of judging everything by our feelings, by *our* comfort, *our* ease, *our* pleasure, *our* freedom from pain. Therein lies the tragedy of living merely natural lives according to the maxims of the world. We misjudge the love of God acting in us, and we repel and insult His love, for it is an insult to murmur against the operations of God's love in us.

How often have we frustrated, literally frustrated, the efforts of God to sanctify us? How often have we repelled Him in the past! Just when His love was sending us, in its most austere but most merciful disguise, the thing that we needed most! For all suffering, no matter how it comes, is God coming to us, is God operating in us. Every suffering that comes to us from contact with creatures has a mission to perform in our soul for God. This mission is to purify us of self-will, to uplift us, to free us from ourselves. It is sent by God and it is our duty to accept it.

When we recall, for example that Saint Vincent DePaul would never have a fire in his room in order that he might accept the cold as God sent it; when we recall that Saint Benedict Labre would permit insects to sting him without brushing them aside, we begin to have a dim view of the tremendous scope there is for the pure and simple acceptance of daily sufferings through which Almighty God comes to purify and sanctify us.

Sanctification and Our Attitude Toward Creatures

So, whether the day be Pentecost or any other day, God the Sanctifier comes to us. He comes to us as He came this day, invisibly, by His grace. He also comes visibly to us through the instrumentality of the creatures with which we come in contact at every single moment. Our contacts with these creatures, which are God's instruments, will produce sanctification in our souls according to our reaction to, according to our attitude towards them.

We are sanctified only when we see and embrace and cling to Him and His will in every single person and thing and circumstance and event in our life. In embracing them, remember that it is His will, and it is His action in us that we must love and embrace, not the evil thing, not the disagreeable thing itself. We must embrace *His will* with our will and our mind. Nothing must be allowed to separate us from His will.

Like Saint Paul, we must be able to say, "I am sure that neither death, nor life, nor angels, nor principalities, nor things present, nor things to come, nor powers, nor height, nor depth nor any other creature will be able to separate us

from the love of God, which is in Christ Jesus our Lord."
"I am *sure*," he said. He could say I am sure because he had
weighed every one of them, things present and things to
come, height and depth, and so on. He had measured them
all with a single eye, the eye of faith, and he saw them all
as *instruments* by which God sanctified him. Therefore, he
was sure that having recognized them as instruments, he
could never be separated from God by them.

To see that fact, to recognize the hand of God in every
person we meet and every event that happens to us, to realize Him in every circumstance of our life is the sum total of
all the gifts of the Holy Ghost that God could give us, because this is one of the greatest truths in the world that we
could know: God is constantly operating *in us* through the
circumstances of our lives, to sanctify us, by emptying us
of self-will in order that we may be filled with Him.

That is how He sanctified Saint Paul and all the saints;
that is how He will sanctify us, by coming to us and operating
in us through the instrumentality of all the creatures with
which we come in contact. If we have been resisting His
sanctifying action, begin now to develop the opposite habit!

CHAPTER X

Abandonment and Our Present State

NOT LONG AGO, at a community retreat house, a director was discussing spiritual direction with one of the Sisters on retreat. She made a highly intelligent and very good spiritual communication. She had isolated her predominant failures, and they discussed the means by which she could plan an attack on those failures, so that she would be able to make some progress against them. The very mental processes involved in discussing those means and the method for implementing them made them appear perhaps somewhat easy to the Sister.

As they talked, the Sister's whole life, so to speak, seemed to light up in her mind. Spiritual desires actually formed in her almost tangibly. Her shoulders went back, and she seemed to be saying interiorly, "Why hadn't I seen all that before? Why didn't I think of this before? It all seems so easy and there is something definite that I have to work on now!" She appeared to be implying: "There will be nothing to this!"

Sister looked off into space for quite a few seconds and then, suddenly, a kind of cloud came over her countenance; her shoulders seemed to sag and she appeared to come back to reality reluctantly, as one would do after having been absorbed in a play or story to such an extent that contact with reality had been lost for a while. Sister summed up the interior conflict that had gone on within her in those few moments by emitting a big sigh, and she said, "It is so easy, at the time of retreat, to think of all the things we would like to do; but it is so hard to go home and do them."

There was an element akin to discouragement in her voice; she seemed almost to have the attitude of being defeated before starting her endeavor. It was not difficult to imagine her thoughts as she saw how far she was from the ideal she had of herself—how far she was from what she would like really to be. This disappointing knowledge seemed to be accentuated by all the reflections that she had had the opportunity to make during the course of the retreat. The thought of her ideal self, of what she would like to be, differed so greatly from what she apparently saw the reality to be, that she was tempted to be discouraged. Moreover, the effort it seemed necessary to expend in order to achieve anything like her ideal seemed so great as to be discouraging.

The Cause of Discouragement

Why, we might ask, was that Sister apparently so discouraged in one moment, when just a few moments before she appeared to have such ideals, such intense desires to overcome her faults and acquire virtues? The reason would seem to be a fault which, unfortunately, is all too often common to everyone of us. She was trusting in herself and not in God; she was hoping in herself instead of in God; she was depending upon herself instead of upon God. Consequently, she was discouraged.

She was, so to speak, being a Pelagian. She fell into the error of Pelagius, a heretic of the fourth century who denied the necessity of grace. He said that a man can fulfill the divine law and conquer all temptations and achieve perfection without the help of grace. While Sister would shrink in horror from such a principle dogmatically, or in the speculative order, she was certainly acting as a Pelagian in the practical order by unconsciously planning her life apart from God's grace and the help of God's grace. Consequently, she was feeling the burden of "playing God" in her own life.

After the big sigh, reference was made again to her statement: "It is so easy to think, at the time of retreat, of the things we would like to do, but so hard to go home and do them." She was asked a question, and it would be well and profitable for us to ask ourselves the same question when we are thinking of the things we would like to do in the spiritual order, the faults we would like to overcome, and the virtues we would like to acquire. It would be beneficial for us to ask, "*Why* would we like to do these things?"

Why Do We Want to Be Better?

Frequently, we should evaluate our *motives* for all the spiritual things we would like to do, overcoming faults, et cetera. In liking to do these things, is God really in our plan? Is His will in our considerations at all? There can be many motives why we might want to do all those things that we "would like to do," many motives why we would want to acquire certain virtues or overcome particular faults. We could want to do so because we would *feel* good about it; we would be able to taste the sweet fruits of success in the spiritual combat. Or, we would like to overcome these faults so that we could *look* good, so that never again would we be embarrassed by having someone see us fall into them; or never again would we be humiliated by being admonished or corrected for the particular fault that weighs us down.

Again, we might want to do all these things so that we could measure up to the ideal that we have of ourself. We might like to overcome these faults so that we would not have to struggle against them anymore, so that we would not have to worry further about reproaching ourself for these failures. Our motive might be to have a kind of peace of mind by being able to look God in the face without having our failure loom up between us.

Again, we might want to be rid of these faults and acquire this particular degree of perfection so that we might reach a plateau where, we hope, we could rest in peace. Once there, we would have this desired virtue automatically; we would not have to worry about striving to practice it. It would be, we think subconsciously, somewhat like a writer learning to type by typing the material he composes. It is easy to imagine his wishing to get rid of the faults that he has in typing, so that when typing becomes a confirmed habit—when he does not have to give it much thought—he can then give all of his thought and effort to his creative writing.

So, it is possible to want to be rid of our faults and to acquire virtue so that having done it, we can rest and be freer to devote our attention to other things. We would then have more time for our duty, or be able to have more concern for our administrative work or hobbies.

All these are possible motives for wanting to do "all the things we would like to do," which we think about at the time of retreat, or at other times of special graces. All of these could be motives for wanting to overcome faults or acquire virtues.

But *none* of them is a true supernatural motive. None of these motives is truly a motive of faith or of love of God, because all the motives mentioned for overcoming our faults leave God out of the picture, or have God only vaguely connected with the goal.

We make a mistake in viewing our own perfection as an objective to be sought apart, somehow, from God—as separate from God—as if our perfection had objective reality independent of God, which, of course, it does not have, nor will it ever have.

Because we fail to see our perfection as being achieved only when we are being absorbed in God, because God is only vaguely connected with our true goal, therefore God's help in achieving that goal is forgotten, is not thought of, is not adverted to. And when God's help is not thought of or adverted to, when it is not constantly in our minds, the inevitable result follows as it followed with Sister. She proved it when she spoke. As soon as she realized it was so "hard to go home and do all the things she would like to do," she became discouraged. The task seemed too great for her because she was depending upon herself.

Sister and we ourselves, in such a situation, are a second edition of Saint Peter walking on the water. Confident, a victim of indiscrete zeal, trusting in himself, he started to climb out of the boat and walk on the water to our Saviour. Our Divine Lord let him fall into the inevitable result of self-trust, which is faint-heartedness and discouragement. Peter began to be afraid of the wind and the waves; he began to sink. Only when he forgot his self-confidence and his trust in himself and his own efforts, and turned to Christ humbly and trustfully, only then was he saved.

So, like Peter, Sister at retreat and we ourselves confidently plan all the things that we would like to do, all the faults that we would like to overcome, the virtues that we would like to acquire. In our Pelagian self-confidence, we decide we are literally going to run on our way to sanctity. But we no sooner have one foot over the gunwale of the boat when we find ourselves beginning to sink. Then we quickly become discouraged.

As with Sister and Saint Peter, so in our case, the only answer to the problem is to confide in God and avoid trusting in ourselves and our own efforts. We must develop absolute confidence in the infinite wisdom and power and goodness of God. He is infinitely wise and He knows what is best for us; He is infinitely good and He wants what is best for us; He is infinitely powerful and He can do and will do what is best for us.

Therefore, the only answer to our difficulty in this problem of our growth in perfection, as in all problems, is to conform to the will of God. For the perfection that we seek and the perfection that God wants for us is nothing other than the union of our wills with His will. It consists only in wanting at every moment what God wants. Behold the essence of perfection: The union of our will with God's will. Perfection will finally be reached when our wills are completely united to and in conformity with God's will at every single moment of our life without exception.

Perfection Is Wanting What Is

We prepare best and most perfectly for union with God in the next moment to come, by accepting completely and absolutely every one of the circumstances of this precise moment now. That very attitude, having our minds and wills united with God, is, in itself, perfection. It is in itself union. Without it, there can be no perfection. There can not be even the seeking of perfection if our wills are not united with God's will. This union of our will with God's will must extend even to the condition of our soul, even to the *degree of perfection* we have reached at any given moment, because all of those circumstances are God's will.

"But suppose I am in sin; suppose I feel miserable?" Well, thank God, then, for the way we feel. For the way we feel, is part of the circumstances of the moment. That circumstance and all other circumstances in the world, from the buzzing of a mosquito's wings to the length of the stride of an ant on the sidewalk are God's will. Therefore, they are the best things that can be at that moment. They reflect God's glory and they work unto good for those who love God who wants things that way at that moment, and has arranged them so. Saint Paul says: "To those who love God all things work together unto good." He says and he means *all* things, the good and the bad and the indifferent! So, in exact proportion to the extent that we want what God wants, including our own spiritual state at this precise moment, our next moment will be better. So, also, we will be better because perfection and holiness are synonymous with union of will with God's will.

"But suppose," we say, "suppose I really want to be a saint; suppose I desire perfection. Shouldn't I be unbearable to myself as I am? Shouldn't things be different from what they are now? How can I be satisfied with what I am now if I want to be a saint?" Well, the answer to that question is both yes and no.

No Limit to Desires and Effort

In our desires for holiness, *yes!* Go as far as we want; go as far as we can. Desire the very stars! Desire to be holy and let our desires carry us into eternity, into the very arms of God himself! In desire, covet as much holiness as we possibly can. In *effort*, also, put forth as much as we can! Strive as much as we are able for holiness; strive as if everything depended upon us, and pray as if everything depended upon God.

But in our *actual will*, here and now, we must want what *is*—now! We must want what is now, because that is what God wants, and that is what God has arranged; otherwise it *could not* be that way. So, no matter what our desires for holiness might be at every given moment, we *are*, in fact, what God has willed us to be.

If now, at four-fifteen, we are what we are, it is God's will.

Thank God for it. *Desire* to be a canonizable saint at five o'clock; *work* with all we have to become a canonizable saint by five o'clock. We may be worse by then than we are now; we may be better. But whatever we are, thank God for it, because that is what God wills; that is what He wants. It is His will; otherwise it could not be that way. But no matter what we are at five o'clock, desire, by six o'clock, to be a saint all over again. If by six, we are much nearer sanctity, then, thank God for that; if not, thank Him also, for that is His will.

Our footsteps along the road to perfection, of course, are bound to lag behind our desires. It cannot help being that way. For example, if we are to make a trip to our home in New York from Baltimore, we are foolish not to desire to reach there; we are foolish if we are not there already in our mind, wishing we were there and thinking of when we shall be there. But the reality is we are still in Baltimore, or near Baltimore, and all the fretting and all the worrying about it in the world won't get us home to New York any faster. It will only distract our attention from the essential business of travel. It hinders our getting there as fast as we otherwise would if we were not worrying.

Conditions are the same on the road to sanctity, on the way to heaven, on the way to holiness! If our desires did not run ahead of our actual steps, we would never reach our goal. But remember this: we *are* on a journey, and we can not get there overnight; it is a lifetime's journey. Each day we should thank God for the progress we have made up to that point. However much we may strain in desire and want to be at the goal, we make each day only the mileage that God would have us make. Today, perhaps, we made only five miles. Tomorrow we might *want* to advance ten miles, but actually we accomplish only two because of the snow of self-will or bad habit. So, independently of our aspirations, wherever we are at any given moment of our journey, we are at the point God wants us to be, plan as we will otherwise. For our progress is according to *God's will* and God's plan, and not according to our own.

We, on our part, must cooperate with God's will and with all His inspirations. We must be led by the Spirit of God. As St. Paul tells us: "Whoever are led by the Spirit of God, they are the sons of God." We must be docile to His directions at every *now*. That is all any of the saints ever did. A saint never wants to advance one step faster or further than God wills; he never wants even to put his foot into heaven before God's sweet Providence would have it so, for the saints lived only in accord with God's Providence and His will.

No Progress without Conformity to God's Will

Perfection necessarily implies our *wanting* to make the progress that *God* would have us make; but this necessarily means we must conform our will to the progress that *we have made at* any given moment of our lives.

That very conformity is a major part of the *progress* that He wants us to make. All contrary thoughts are merely manifestations of the impatience of our own will to have God hasten our journey to holiness according to *our own* ideas, instead of according to His plan. This, be it noted well, is one of Satan's most subtle temptations with which he tries to delude those who are striving to be holy and who are really seeking perfection.

As long as he can keep them stirred up and *unconformed* to God's will, at least in the matter of their spiritual state at any given moment, to that extent he has dis-united them from God's will; to that extent they have failed to reach the perfection that God would have them reach, because perfection consists in uniting our will with God's will in everything, including our degree of perfection, even though we with our puny minds can not see the wisdom of what God wills.

So, in summary, what God wants of us is to want what *is*. In particular, God wants us to want what *is* in regard to our spiritual state because whatever that is, is God's will, unless we be in sin. Even in that event, the guilt of that sin is His permissive will from which He intends to draw greater good by our repentence. Those who want everything, every single thing, every single circumstance, every single action, above all, every thing about their spiritual state exactly as it is now, at this moment, because God has arranged it so, *they* are the saints.

Objection: Why Try?

But an answer must be given now to an objection that might occur to many: Because God has willed that I be what I am now, and holiness consists in my wanting that, does it mean that I must want to *stay* the way I am now? God forbid! As has been said, it merely means that God wants me to be what I am *now* and therefore I must thank Him for it. But that is *this now*. I do not know yet what He wants me to be the *next now*. The *next* now, He may want me to be something completely different. I know with certainty that He wants me to *try* to be something better the next now, for He has said, "Be ye holy because I am holy." Again, He said, "Be ye perfect as your Heavenly Father is perfect." Again, "This is the will of God, your sanctification."

But, the objection continues, if we *will be* what God wants us to be at any given moment, what is the use of our trying to be more perfect? Such a question is reminiscent of the Pilgrim father who was starting out through the woods without his gun. His wife remonstrated at his temerity, pointing out that he might be killed by Indians. He answered that if God willed him to be killed, he would be killed whether he had his gun or not. To which his wife replied: "But suppose God wills you to be killed on condition that you don't have your gun with you?" In her wisdom, she knew that God wills some things absolutely and other things He wills *conditionally*. The condition, in many instances, is something that depends on us, such as our prayers, or our acting in a certain way. Thus, we *must try* to be perfect because that is God's will for us. We know with certainty that unless we *try* to be perfect, we can not be united with His will at all.

Therefore, this doctrine is in no wise a case of fatalism or quietism. Catholic teaching is that whatever *is*, whatever *has happened* is God's will, with the sole exception of the guilt of sin, which is His permissive will. Otherwise, whatever is could not have happened, for God is the universal cause of all things, except for the guilt of sin. But it is also true that no perfection is possible without doing God's will. And His will is that we *strive* each moment to *be* better, as has just been said above.

Consequently, thanking God for what we are now does not mean that we want to *stay* what we are now. It does not, above all, mean that we *can* stay such with impunity. We must *want* to be better the next now, and we must *work* to be better. God will give us the grace to be better, to be completely different. We must strive to cooperate with that grace as much as we possibly can. But, the next hour from now we must again rejoice in what we are at that now. And so on to the following *now*, and the succeeding *now;* always, at every now, our will must be completely united with the will of God for all time and for eternity.

Therefore, as has been said, things can not be different from what they are at any given now, or moment, because they are the way that God has arranged them. To want what God wants, particularly for ourself, is to fulfill the counsel to cast our cares upon the Lord. Behold the secret of true peace and true happiness: To want *everything* about the *now* that is, and particularly the now as regards ourself, because it is what God wants!

Heaven on Earth

To want what we are *now,* and to strive to be a saint in the *next* moment; and as the next now comes along, to want what is at *that new* now, but strive to be better the *following* now—what is that but the finding of heaven right here on earth. For what is heaven? Heaven is where there is no past, or no future, but only the present, an endless, eternal, infinite succession of nows—now—now—now—in which our will will be completely united with the will of God.

We have it, then, within our power to live our heaven right here on earth. We do that as often as, and as long as, at each successive now, we want what God wants for others and for ourselves. Want what is now, but be infinite in our desires for perfection at the next moment, and when the next moment comes, want what is then, because that is what God wants; *that* is casting our cares on the Lord; that is the recipe for enjoying the peace that surpasses understanding.

CHAPTER XI

Weekly Confession

A QUESTION THAT MUST occur to all periodically is this: "Why am I not better?" When we think of all of the aids we have in living our spiritual life, it would seem that we should make more rapid progress. Consider one of these aids, the Sacrament of Penance, which we have at our disposal week after week, and which should contribute to our constant spiritual improvement. Very often, we find it does not produce that result. We might ask ourselves why this is so.

Perhaps a clue to the answer might be found in the parable which our Divine Lord told about the sower going out to sow his seed. Some fell by the wayside; and some on stony ground; and some on thorns, and so on. But He said, "Some fell upon good ground and brought forth fruit, some a hundred-fold, some sixty-fold, and some thirty-fold." Now, note that all the latter was *good ground,* and yet it brought forth varying degrees of fruit. So, too, our souls are essentially good ground for the reception for the Sacrament of Penance; we have the essential dispositions to receive the sacrament validly and licitly. Yet, because of defects of our disposition, we do not receive the hundred-fold of fruit that we might receive and that our Lord wants us to receive from our weekly confession.

Purpose of the Sacrament of Penance

So, then, importance must be attached to the answer to the question: "How can we derive more profit from our weekly confessions?" First of all, we must be clear on the purpose of the Sacrament of Penance in relation to God's plan for us and our holiness. God's plan for our sanctification consists essentially in His raising us to the supernatural state of adopted sonship by uniting us to the Mystical Body of His Son. From our union with the Mystical Body, we participate in and live with the life of God called sanctifying grace. We are likewise assured of the actual graces necessary to live the supernatural life. As a consequence, we have the power, in every moment of earthly life, to glorify God on earth and to increase our supernatural capacity to glorify Him forever in heaven and consequently to enjoy His happiness forever there. The only thing that can interfere with God's plan for us, and consequently the only real evil in the world, is sin. Mortal sin completely destroys God's plan for us, and venial sin interferes with its perfect accomplishment.

But God in his goodness was not content to let us run the risk of losing His incomparable gift of supernatural life forever, through our own foolishness, by mortal sin. To prevent this, He devised a second plank of salvation, as the Fathers of the Church called it, a means of sanctification and salvation having a two-fold end. It would be the means whereby, if we had the misfortune to lose the supernatural life by mortal sin, we could regain it; and it would also be the means whereby we could, while still retaining it, grow and increase in the supernatural life. That means is the Sacrament of Penance.

Our Divine Saviour in His goodness instituted Penance

to be a sacrament of peace. He intended the sacrament of forgiveness to be a means of peace for souls troubled by failure in their efforts to love and serve Him. Consequently, anyone who foolishly makes the Sacrament of Penance anything but a sacrament of peace is using it contrary to the intentions and purposes of our Divine Saviour. When we approach confession, we do not go before a prosecuting attorney. It is the only court in the world in which the defendant is his own accuser.

Above all, we should remember that in this sacrament we appear before a kind and loving and merciful judge who is anxious and willing to forgive us. Each time we go to confession, we offer God an opportunity to exercise His greatest prerogative which, Saint Thomas tells us, is His mercy, an attribute even greater, in a certain sense, than his justice.

In considering the Sacrament of Penance from a practical point of view, and with the purpose of making its weekly reception a more productive factor for good in our spiritual life, it is convenient to divide it into three distinct parts, or three different actions on the part of the penitent, who is our concern in this place.

Examination of Conscience

The first act of the penitent, in chronological order, is the preparation for confession called the examination of conscience. Before beginning this examination, we should ask Almighty God to give us a knowledge of our sins and a hatred of them such as He has. Beg Him to give us the grace to see sin, and especially our own sins, as He sees them.

This cannot be done, of course, in a few minutes after rushing to the chapel from some absorbing occupation when we hear a bell ring to announce confession time. We cannot, it is true, always choose the time we would like to go to confession, and sometimes we do not know when the confessor is coming. But, if such is our chronic situation, we should make our preparation for confession at some time we do have available, even if it be the night before our confession day, presuming there be no time on the day of confession itself. But no matter when we do it, it certainly seems that fifteen minutes is not too much time to devote to preparation for such an important sacrament as the Sacrament of Penance.

While we are examining our conscience, two extremes are to be avoided. One is to be slipshod, and the other is to be scrupulous. A good rule of thumb is never to use more than half the time of preparation for confession in examining our conscience. Generally, if we go to confession regularly, some five minutes is sufficient to examine our conscience for a weekly confession. In fact, one of the saints used to say there were two things we should be ready for at any moment: death and confession. If Religious go to confession weekly, as required by Canon law, and carry out faithfully the particular examination, surely five minutes would suffice for examination of conscience. But, in any case, it should never be protracted more than half the time of our preparation for confession.

In the actual process of examining our conscience, having prayed to the Holy Spirit for light, we should look first of all for mortal sins. This, of course, is not generally a state-wide manhunt for which we have to organize a posse. If, God forbid, there be any mortal sins on the soul of a Religious, they are not hidden away in a corner under the dust. They are prominent in red and blue neon. Moreover, they are flashing on and off in our attention. We know they are there without having to look for them.

But if, please God, there be no mortal sins, we then look for the venial sins we have committed since our last confession. We look particularly for *deliberate* venial sins, and more particularly, for deliberate venial sins against the greatest of the virtues and consequently the most grave of venial sins in themselves, namely, venial sins against charity. We look for venial sins against charity in speech, in thought, in action. Then we look for deliberate sins against the duties of our state in life, as defined in our holy rules, particularly those against obedience and abandonment as we saw in the chapter on our predominant fault.

In searching for these venial sins, we should look for the ones that are the most serious, the ones that stand most in the way of our progress. It is not necessary, of course, in examining our conscience, to go over every thought that we have had since last week, every person we have spoken to, every place we went, and everything we did, trying to think up an interminable list of peccadillos, and sins and failings.

There are those who make the examination of conscience a "tour de force" of their memory, a sheer, brilliant exhibition of the ability of the human mind to recall, like Univac, everything they might have done since their last confession. They may arrange their sins in logical order, or in numerical order, or some original order of their own conceiving. When, at the end of examination time, the memorization is complete, they come in breathless to the confessional, the priest opens the slide and they sputter their list like a fourth of July sparkler burning out. Their memory feat endures just about as long as the ephemeral sparkler. Once it has sputtered out, it is gone, never more to be rekindled. But the worry about it is not gone. Leaving the confessional, such penitents begin to wonder if they told them all, how many did they forget, and were they all understood just as they were in reality.

All such straining is, of course, completely foreign to and a travesty on the wonderful memorial of the mercy of God which is the Sacrament of Penance. God is not interested in multiple computations. The faculty which must operate to obtain pardon is not our memory but our will. God forgives us our sins not because we remember them well, but because we are sorry for them in our will.

Being Sorry for Sin

Hence, after examining our conscience, the major portion of the time of preparation for confession should be devoted to the most important part of our weekly confession. What is that? Let us highlight it in this way: There are circumstances in which our sins can be forgiven without examining our conscience. For example, if we were walking on the avenue and were struck unconscious by a car, a priest could give us absolution and forgive our sins, even though we did not examine our conscience at all. As a matter of fact we could not do so because we were unconscious.

Again, there are circumstances in which our sins can be forgiven without confessing them. Soldiers going into battle can not possibly have time to go to confession. Yet, the chaplain can give them absolution "in globo," as it is called, and their sins are forgiven, if they are sorry for them and intend to confess them when they have an opportunity. Or, to refer again to our previous case, if we are unconscious, we can not confess our sins, but still they can be forgiven.

So, it can be said that there are circumstances in which sins can be forgiven without examining our conscience; there are circumstances in which sins can be forgiven without our confessing them. But there are no circumstances under God's blue heaven in which our sins can be forgiven without our *being sorry for them.* Here we have touched the very heart of the Sacrament of Penance, the most important part, namely, *contrition.* We must be sorry for our sins if we are to have them forgiven.

But please note well precisely what has been said: We

must *be* sorry; not we must *feel* sorry. These are two vastly different acts.

Feeling sorry is in the emotions, in the feelings. We could feel more sorry about seeing a cute little puppy run over and hurt in the street than about the gravest confession we ever made. That is, we could feel greater sorrow in the sensible order, manifested by the shedding of tears and other signs. That would be *feeling* sorry; but that is not what God asks of us in regard to sin. We must *be* sorry; and being sorry is not in the emotions but in the will. *Being* sorry for our sins means that we hate the sin we have committed and have a firm determination not to commit sin again. The essence of sorrow is the regret or hatred of the evil we have done accompanied by the firm determination, with God's help, of not committing it again.

Obviously, the sincerity of our sorrow, when we come out of confession, is found by asking ourselves what we have resolved not to do again. Suppose a companion were to walk up to us and slap us in the face and say, "I am sorry, dear, I didn't mean it." But, if at the time of the apology, we knew that the next time we met coming around the corner that companion intended to slap us again, we would not think much of the sorrow. So, too, when we kneel down and tell our Lord that we are sorry for having slapped Him in the face, that we are sorry for having hurt Him, if He can read in our hearts that the next time we get the same occasion, we will not resist any harder than we did in the past, then, He does not think much of our sorrow.

Father Nash, S.J., somewhere in his writings gives an example to show the futility of such sorrow. Following his thought, let us picture Christ, after his scourging, sitting in the courtyard of Pilate, the drunken rabble and the soldiers mocking Him. See Him there, clothed in an old purple rag with a crown of thorns on His head, a reed sceptre in His hand. See the drunken soldiers with their mailed fists coming up and slapping Him, then genuflecting and spitting at Him and railing at Him, between swigs out of a bottle. Poor, gentle Christ! Then imagine one soldier stepping forward from that crowd, reeling toward Christ. Suddenly a hush comes over them all. They fall back afraid, wondering. They watch breathlessly as they see that big burly soldier go up and kneel down before the gentle Christ with an apparent change of heart. They hear him say, "Master, I am sorry for my part in this. I am truly sorry." Then, when the hush has completely subdued the crowd, imagine him standing up completely, wiping his mouth with the back of his hand and then hauling off and striking Christ across the face again, laughing jeeringly, and getting the others to join in the laugh at his mock sorrow.

Just the relation of such an incident strikes horror into our hearts. Yet, is that not precisely what we do when we go to confession to tell our Lord we are sorry, and at the same time have no intention of ever doing anything about that antipathy, about that unkindness, about that uncharitable speech, about that impatience, about that bitterness? We tell Him we are sorry; we pretend that we are sorry, but in reality we have no intention in the world of doing anything to change; for all practical purposes we intend continuing to do the same thing over again.

Yet, unless we are sorry for our sins and intend, with God's help, to do what we can to avoid them in the future, they are not and can not be forgiven. Thus it can be possible to confess venial sins and not have them forgiven, because we are not sorry for them.

We can be sorry and be as fearful as we will that we *might* fall in the future; but the purpose of amendment means that here and now, our intention and our resolution is, with God's help, to do everything possible to try not to commit this sin again. We will use all the means necessary not to fall into this deliberate sin again.

It is not difficult to stir up such sorrow in our hearts and wills if we only think of the motives that we have for being sorry. If anyone in the world had done as much for us as our Lord has, and we continued to treat him with the same coldness and contempt and indifference that we show our Lord, we would not have a friend in the world. We would not be able to look ourself in the face with any respect. In a word, the crucifix, the passion of Christ, is the greatest motive in the world to stir up true sorrow for our sins.

Since *being* sorry for our sins is the most important part of our weekly confessions, we should spend the greater part of our time of preparation for confession in stirring up this sorrow. The *act* of contrition, the act of sorrow that we make during the actual administration of the Sacrament of Penance is merely an external *sign* to the confessor that we are sorry. The only way he has of judging our sorrow is by that act of contrition. He has to take our word that we mean it. It is an external sign to him that we are sorry. But if we wait to get into the confessional before we try to arouse our sorrow, then the distractions of listening to the absolution or thinking about what penance the priest has given us, and so on, make very poor circumstances in which to stir up real, true sorrow for our sins. Hence, the wisdom of *being* sorry *before* we enter the confessional, for it is the most important part of penance. Hence, the importance of asking Almighty God for the grace of sorrow while assisting at Mass on the morning of the day we go to confession.

The true sorrow we arouse for our sins at examination time does not, of course, militate in any way against our thanking God for the fact that we are not much worse than we are, that we do not have worse things to confess than we have. It recognizes that God's grace and God's goodness alone have prevented us from falling even lower. If we are troubled and upset at seeing ourselves down, that upset is not from love of God; it is from love of self. If we really knew ourselves as we are, if we were truly humble, instead of being surprised at seeing ourselves down, we would wonder how we were ever erect.

The third act of the penitent after the examination of conscience and the stirring up of contrition for our sins is *confession*, the actual telling of our sins to the priest. In this, all God asks is that we be sincere, that we accuse ourselves as we know ourselves to be before Him. This can be done without difficulty if we exercise our faith and recall to whom it is that we are confessing our sins. We are confessing our sins to God, to our divine Lord, through His representative, the priest. We are confessing our sins to Christ who already knows them better than we do. He knows in what we are guilty. He knows our weakness; He knows our heart and He knows our record. We cannot deceive Him. It is so much easier to confess our sins if we keep in mind that we are speaking to our Divine Lord Himself who already knows our hearts and what we have done, and who has decreed that we humble ourselves by telling our sins to Him through the ears of one of his ministers.

It helps, further, to remember that the priest, the representative of our Lord to whom we confess, does not know us, and that no matter whose confession he hears, he knows that there, but for the grace of God, goes he. He is a human being like his penitents. He does not know us and even if he did know us, he has the grace of office by which, once he walks out of the confessional, he can ignore whatever he has heard. The good Lord knows he has problems enough of his own without carrying ours around with him.

Furthermore, after his study of theology and human nature, and his years of experience in dealing with sinful humanity, after what he knows of his own heart and his own weakness, if we think that a "Johnny or Jenny-come-lately" like us is going to disclose a new kind of sin that will literally knock him off his chair, we are very foolish. Yet, that is the way the devil can work on us at times. So very often, he takes away peoples' shame when he induces them to commit sin, then gives it back to them when it is time to confess it. Succumbing to that shame, they conceal its cause in confession and thus they make a very sad and tragic mistake.

Telling What We Are

As a beneficial refinement of the confession of our venial sins, it is much better to reveal, not so much what we did, as what we *are*. So often, we say: "I was disobedient." That is *what* we did, but do we ever tell *why* we were disobedient? It could be for many reasons. We were proud; because we were arrogant; because we were moved habitually by human respect. Again, we might say, "I was uncharitable." That is what we did, but what we *are* is, again, self-opinionated, attached to our own judgement, intolerant of any opposition.

When we are confessing our venial sins thus, when we take the trouble to try to discover and to mention the cause, the root fault that underlies the surface rash, we produce a two-fold beneficial effect. First of all, we realize more vividly our sins and their intrinsic nature and evil and are thus more strongly motivated to avoid routine in confessing them and to struggle more courageously against them. By confessing the underlying causes of our external faults, we likewise invite direction from the confessor who, seeing that we care enough about our own advancement to use some means to achieve it, is moved to interest himself and apply his efforts to the same end.

What We Should Confess

Having treated of the manner of making actual confession, the interesting question remains: What *should* we confess? But even anterior to that, we should know what we *must* confess. That is, what do we have an obligation to confess? For our peace of mind, it should be recalled that all we *have* to confess, all that anybody has to confess, all that there is an obligation to confess is the number and kinds of mortal sins that one is certain he has committed. That is all! The only thing that we have an obligation to confess are mortal sins that we know with certainty we have committed, along with their number and kind.

Any youngster in catechism class knows that for mortal sin there must be present grievous matter, sufficient reflection, and full consent of the will. We must be dealing with some act or omission gravely sinful; we must know what we are doing and do it despite its sinfulness. That is a mortal sin. Sins of that kind are all that we have an obligation to confess. Other kinds of sins we do not have to confess. We may; it is often well to; but we do not have to.

Here, incidentally, a word of caution is in order. When it is said that mortal sin requires grievous matter, sufficient reflection or knowledge, and full consent of the will, the knowledge in question must be had at the time we commit the sin, *not later*. Suppose that five years ago we committed a sin, and at *that time* we did not know the act was sinful, or, at least, we did not think it was mortally sinful. Now, five years later we learn that what we did five years ago was, in fact, a mortal sin. Sometimes one concludes: "My, I did that, maybe several times, and I never told it in confession. Therefore, I have been making bad confessions all these years." Then begins the big worry! But such worry is useless and wrong.

It is wrong for this reason. Any subsequent knowledge we acquire about an act that we did in the past does not change at all what we thought about it at the past time, nor any guilt that was then incurred. If we did something yesterday and we did not think it was a mortal sin, but tomorrow we learn it was mortal, still, for *us* that particular act was *not* a mortal sin at the time we did it. On the other hand, if we did this something yesterday and we thought it *was* a mortal sin, but tomorrow we learn that it is *not* a mortal sin, then, for *us* it *was* a mortal sin at the time we did it. This is so because we are judged according to what we do with what we know. Hence, as we learn more and more about the spiritual life and the virtues, let us not foolishly stampede into worry and concern because of new things we learn about old things we did in the past. God judges us only on what we do with what we know.

While on the subject of doubt, it is well to recall that doubtful sins are not matter for absolution. If we do not know whether we consented to such and such a sin, then, for us it is not a sin. We may, for peace of mind, confess such as a doubtful sin. For example, we can say: "I do not know whether I gave in to this, or whether I was fully voluntary in doing this, but I would like to confess it as it is before God." We may do that, but we should never confess doubtful sin as certain, or by the same token, certain sin as doubtful.

Returning to the question of *what* we should confess, it is clear that all we *have* to confess are the number and kinds of mortal sins. But if, please God, we have no mortal sins to confess and want to receive sacramental absolution and the grace of the sacrament, we have to confess at least one venial sin. The reason is that the Sacrament of Penance is a judgement made on sin and can not, therefore, take place unless a sin is confessed. But, no doubt, every one of us, if we search our hearts and our reins sufficiently deep, can find at least one venial sin which can be matter for absolution and reception for the graces of the sacrament. The venial sin we confess can be of our present or past life, that is either already forgiven or not.

Saint Vincent DePaul advises us never to confess more

than two venial sins or three at the most. The reason is the difficulty of having specific sorrow for, and making resolutions about, and being determined to avoid even that many in the future. Thus, he tells us to concentrate on two or three. It would be most difficult to have firm resolutions of amendment about long enumerations of venial sins, week after week. Furthermore, any venial sins for which we are truly sorry are forgiven in confession even if we do not confess them.

Thus, among those two or three venial sins told in our weekly confession, we should mention those about which we took resolutions in our confession last week. Above all and before all, we should confess the sins of our predominant failing upon which we are working for our practice. As mentioned in the chapter on the particular examen, we should make that sin part of the matter of our weekly confession, in fact the focal point of it. Whether it be ambition, or pride, or sensitiveness, or whatever it might be, we should confess that sin each week along with its causes, trying to cut down the number of times, the number of occasions on which we fall into it. If last week we confessed that we fell eight times, we should resolve that with the help of God next week it be down to four. When next week comes, we might have to say seven or even nine times. No matter! At confession, we tell God we are sorry and take a *new* resolution for the following week. The grace of the absolution will strengthen our resolution and give us additional help to keep it for the succeeding week.

At the end of confession, we should always mention some sin of our past life. The reason is that we will thus be sure to have sufficient matter for confession. Secondarily, but also importantly, it is an act of humiliation. That it may be truly salutary from the penitential viewpoint, we should pick out some sin of our past life that we might be ashamed or embarrassed or humiliated to tell. Such confession is a good act of penance in itself, and at confession we are in the Sacrament of Penance the best place to do penance.

Extraordinary Confession

Before concluding these remarks on what we should confess, there remains a further aspect of the Sacrament of Penance that is frequently puzzling to neophytes in the spiritual life. Perhaps it can best be expressed in the immortal words of one modern postulant who, shortly after her entrance, floored her Mistress with this question: "What's the story on this extraordinary confession deal?" Well, the purpose of an extraordinary confessor being made available once every three months to religious women and certain other categories is, first of all, to give them an opportunity to go to a different confessor who might not otherwise be available. It is not meant to provide an opportunity for them to exercise their memory or to try to recall every sin they might have committed since their last extraordinary confession three months ago.

Perhaps extraordinary confession can best be compared to a business man taking periodic inventory of his affairs. It is an occasion to step back and get an over-all view of ourselves, to see whether we have progressed or gone backward during the past three months. The way we discover that is not by trying to remember whether it was 159 or 184 times we were uncharitable, or whether it was 136 or 127 times that we were impatient, and so on. That is not the purpose of extraordinary confession.

The important thing at extraordinary as at regular confession time is not so much to tell what we *did* but what we *were*. In our examen, we should ask ourselves: "How was I for the last three months? What were the important trends in my life? Did I tend to be progressively more moody? Or, was I getting progressively more impetuous, or impatient? Or did I find myself becoming more and more critical and uncharitable over the past three months?" Thus we sketch our status in broad, bold strokes for our own information, first of all, and then for our confessor. Our chief aim should be to tell him what we *were* during the interval since the last extraordinary confession.

The great spiritual advantage for us in this, besides the grace of the sacrament, is that we have a chance and a reminder to reset our compass again, particularly with regard to the resolutions we took in our annual retreat. Extraordinary confession is the time to check up again on the resolutions we made and wrote down at our annual retreat. We check to see how we are living up to those ideals we proposed to ourselves then, and where we have failed. It is a quarter-annual inventory. Thus, "this extraordinary confession deal," is not at all meant to be a feat of memorizing everything that we told in all the intervening confessions, but an attempt to tell the confessor what we were over the past three months.

Thanksgiving after Confession

After our confession, whether weekly or extraordinary, when we have left the confessional, we should never let it be said of us what our Divine Saviour was forced to say of the ten lepers: "Were not the ten made clean? . . . Has no one been found to return and give glory to God except this foreigner?" When our Divine Lord absolves us of our sins in the confessional, He does something far more wonderful than He did when He cleansed the lepers of their leprosy. That was merely a physical disease, whereas in confession something supernatural takes place—the forgiving of sins, a greater thing, says Saint Augustine, than the creation of the world.

Our thanksgiving will consist, first of all, in devoutly

saying our penance. We must never forget that the simple little penance which the priest gives us has a value in reparation far exceeding what those same prayers would have if we merely chose to say them as a penance ourselves. When we say the penance imposed upon us by the priest in confession, the merits of the passion and death of Christ accompany it and plead with the Father for the remission of the temporal punishment due to our sins. There is tremendous reparatory value to those prayers because of the fact that they are assigned as penance in the Sacrament of Penance.

After we have said our penance, continuing our thanksgiving, our minds will be occupied with thoughts of the goodness of God and of our desire not to sin again, and our determination to die to sin. For example, suppose we had deliberately offended in a cantankerous moment some one we loved very much, maybe one of our companions. Later, we repented of it and went to ask pardon, to say how sorry we were. Suppose she received us most graciously, told us to forget about it, that she would never think of it again, that she did not want us to think of it again, and that things were just as they always were between us. As we arose and left her presence, what do we suppose our thoughts would be? We would be thinking of what a wonderful person she was, how good and how kind and how Christlike, and of how miserable we felt for having hurt her and offended her, and how we were going to make it our business to see that we never did such a thing again.

When we sin, we offend Almighty God who loves us more than anyone in the world can possibly love us. We offend Him whom we want to love. Therefore, when He has forgiven us in confession, when He has told us to forget about it, not to think of it again, if we have any sensitivity, any love for Him at all, our thoughts will follow the same vein. We'll be thinking of His goodness to us; we'll be thinking of trying to make it up to Him, trying to see that we do not offend Him like that again. We will be thinking of ways in which we can pay the debt of temporal punishment which still remains to be paid even after He has forgiven our sins.

As the saintly Abbot Marmion suggests, what better way to pay this debt of temporal punishment than to offer, through the Sacrament of Penance we have just received, all of our acts of mortification and renunciation and penance of the coming week in order that we may die more and more to sin. In this way, we make the fruits of our confession extend throughout the whole week. We increase the value of those acts of penance. We say to our Divine Lord: "Dear Jesus I offer You all the acts of mortification, of renunciation and penance that I am going to do this week, whether voluntary or imposed by rule. I offer them all to You to make it up to You for the sins which You have just forgiven me, and in order to pay part of my debt for the temporal punishment due to my sins which will one day hinder and delay my seeing You." Isn't it wonderful that God in his goodness will accept those pitiful little acts of penance that we do, will accept our offering of them to pay our debt of temporal punishment due to our sins!

The Prayer after Absolution

But there is something more wonderful still. How good God is! Not only does he *accept* such an offering but in the Sacrament of Penance which we have just received, God actually gives a *special value* to such an offering. Because of the fact that the Sacrament of Penance is administered in Latin, we may be unfamiliar with and hence miss the significance of a prayer which the priest says immediately after giving the penance and the words of absolution.

The conclusion of that prayer is: "May whatever good you do, and whatever evil you bear, be to you for the remission of sins, for the increase of grace, and the reward of eternal life."

That prayer is a kind of sacramental since it is established by the Church as a means to obtain grace for us. By it, the priest actually and officially unites to the sacrament we have just received all of our suffering, all of our acts of penance, and mortification, and expiation, and renunciation, and satisfaction. He gives them a special sacramental worth far above what they would have if our acts of penance were not thus joined to the Sacrament of Penance, because now they are sacramental things. Augmenting the value of our own acts of penance, we have the united prayers of the Church, the Mystical Body of Christ pleading before the throne of God, through the little acts of penance which we do.

. . . For the Remission of Sins

More wonderul still, not only does God accept the *voluntary* acts of penance which we do, and the penances which the priest *assigns* to us, but he also gives a special value to all the adversities and hardships and crosses of life which come to us *unlooked* for. "May whatever of good you do, whatever of *evil you bear*, be to you for the remission of sins, the increase of grace, and the reward of eternal life." Therefore, during the course of the week, whenever somebody interrupts us, or annoys us, or is importunate in demands on our time, we can recall our previous confession. We can rejoice that in that confession God gave us special added *value* to the bearing of this cross over and above what our bearing it alone without that sacrament would have. Whenever anybody ignores us, or gives us a short answer, or is ungrateful, or hurts us, or ridicules us, think back to the day of our confession. At that time God gave this cross a special value to do away with the temporal punishment due to our sins; a special value to make up for all the times that we have hurt others, for all the times that we have been unkind, for all the times we have been uncharitable, and inconsiderate, and thoughtless, and lacking in understanding. Whenever we have to bear fatigue, or adverse weather, or an ailment—headache, backache, or any sort of physical adversity, think that God, in our confession, has given these things a special sacramental value to do away with the temporal punishment due to our sins which will one day delay our seeing Him face to face until it is paid in full.

Therefore, in our thanksgiving after confession, we should voluntarily accept and offer to God all of the crosses of sufferings and loneliness and disappointment and hardships of the coming week. We should offer them to God because He has given a special value to them as a result of the prayer which His Church prays for us in the Sacrament of Penance. If we do this, it will spell death to any such thing as routine in our weekly confessions. They will become a vital factor in our lives. We shall be aware, day after day, in our duty and in our community life, of the wonderful thing that has happened to us when we went to confession. We shall be constantly reminded that the priest in addition to forgiving our sins in confession, puts a special *bonus,* so to speak, on whatever good we do, or of evil we bear by, remitting temporal punishment due to our sins.

. . . For the Increase of Grace

Then he says, "May it be to you . . . for the *increase of grace.*" When we were absolved and received the Sacrament of Penance, we received a tremendous flow of sacramental grace into our souls, just as we do when we go to Holy Communion. Remember that that is one of the effects of the Sacrament of Penance. It is not merely an eraser to clean off a blackboard; not merely a kind of laundry. It is a sacramental source of grace like Holy Communion and all of the sacraments, with its own proper effects. It is a way of supernatural growth.

In addition to the increase of sanctifying grace, we receive also particular sacramental graces of the Sacrament of Penance. These are actual graces to be sorry for our past sins, and the right to actual graces to avoid sin in the future. Every time we go to confession, we receive, so to speak, a spiritual battery charge, a new source of power to avoid or combat temptations in the future. We receive graces that we would not have received if we had not received that particular sacrament.

Since, at each confession, God gives us a right to actual graces at the time of temptation, we should never, never miss an opportunity for weekly confession. We should regard it as unthinkable as sitting in chapel at Mass and not going to Holy Communion because we were too lazy to make the effort. Holy Communion is a sacrament and so is penance. Let us never miss an opportunity to receive that grace weekly at least.

If, for any reason, there is no opportunity to get to confession one week, and we find ourselves two weeks away, by the end of that two weeks we are surprized perhaps, to find out how much more difficult it is to triumph over our faults; we become aware that we are slipping more and more easily. For that reason the code of Canon Law imposes an obligation on Religious to go to confession every week. This obligation does not bind them under the pain of sin each week, it being a directive law; but, nevertheless, it is the law that Religious should go to confession every week.

Realizing the great source of grace that is the Sacrament

of Penance, we can appreciate more the bonus, so to speak, that we receive when the priest says, in effect, in his concluding prayer, "May whatever of good that you do," from the time that you get up in the morning until you go to bed at night, and "whatever evil you bear," during the course of that time, "may they be to you for an *increase of grace*" and a consequent death to sin.

. . . For the Reward of Eternal Life

Finally, he says: May these things "be to you for the *reward of eternal life.*" May whatever of good you do, may whatever of evil you bear, *increase* your capacity to enjoy the happiness of heaven and to glorify God forever in heaven. This is the goal of everything; this is what makes everything we might have to bear on earth worth while. Our Divine Lord tells us that if we take up our cross we can be His disciple and we can be with Him in paradise, not, perhaps, on this day, but on the last day, and "your heart shall rejoice, and your joy no one shall take from you."

Thus, as with so many other spiritual problems, the answer to increasing the fruits of our weekly confession is to arouse our faith in what happens there. The Curé of Ars summed it up by saying that when we go to confession, we should be mindful that we are about to take Christ down from the cross. We are about to take the nails out of His hands and His feet, to lower Him gently in our arms, remove the crown of thorns from His head and rest it on our breast to try to comfort Him. When we go to confession, we are making God happy because we are giving Him an opportunity to exercise his greatest attribute, His mercy.

Every time we go to confession, even though we confess only venial sins, the precious blood of Jesus is offered again to the Father for our individual pardon and our individual forgiveness. Every time that God absolves us through the lips of His priest in confession, it is as though all of the suffering and all of the merits, all of the blood of Christ, all of the love of Christ were offered again to His heavenly Father and applied to our individual soul. To stir up our faith in that fact at confession not only pleases God mightily, but also prevents anything like routine creeping into our confession.

Everytime we go to confession, we should strive to put ourselves in the disposition we would want to have if it were the last confession we were to make; we should strive to make it as we would want to make it were God to call us immediately after the sacrament or before we have a chance to go again.

If we do this, we shall walk into the confessional each week conscious that our Divine Lord Himself, at that moment, is offering to His Father again the last drop of His Precious Blood, all the merits of His passion and death for *us* and for the remission of *our* sins. We shall be conscious that the Most Blessed Trinity is occupied with *us* at that moment, as if we were the only soul in the world. We shall be aware that as Christ is forgiving us, so also the Father forgives us, and is about to send the Holy Spirit into our souls with new graces, and that, consequently, God Himself is about to dwell in us with new intensity. This is the glory and the splendor that can be our weekly confession!

CHAPTER XII

Purity of Intention

"WHATEVER YOU DO, work at it from the heart as for the Lord and not for men, knowing that from the Lord you will receive the inheritance as your reward" (Colossians 3:23). The purity of intention which Saint Paul here recommends to us, and which determines the value and merit of our actions and the extent of our reward, can be described very simply as having one aim, one intention, and one motive in everything we do, namely, to please God. Purity of intention is the manifestation of the virtue of simplicity. We can always remember what simplicity is, practically speaking, if we remember the word, *aim;* A, one aim; I, one intention; M, one motive. Purity of intention implies one aim, one intention, and one motive, namely, to please God.

Our Divine Lord has said, "If thy eye be evil, thy whole body will be full of darkness." The figure which our Lord uses here is rather strange sounding to our ears. However, by the eye He means the intention of an action; and by the body He means the action itself. Therefore, if the intention of an action is good, the action, He says, will be good; and if the intention for which we do an action is bad, then the action itself will be bad.

But there are degrees of purity of intention. Our intention is the purer the less there is of self and self-will in our reason or motive for doing things. So, the purer our intention is, the more meritorious our actions are and the more glory do they give to God.

A Christian lives, or should live, for that very purpose. That is the primary reason for which all creation was made —to give glory to God. He made us for Himself, that is, that we might glorify Him and that we might participate in His happiness, which participation is a consequence of our glorifying Him. Saint Paul tells us, "Whether you eat or drink, or do anything else, do all for the glory of God." If we do that, we merit the peace that surpasses understanding, the peace that God decrees and gives as a result of living as we were meant to live and fulfilling the purpose of our existence, that peace which is the tranquility of proper order.

Peace, then, is the result of striving to please God and not other people or ourselves. By working with purity of intention, we give glory to God, we bring happiness to the angels and the saints and our Divine Lord in heaven. "There will be joy in heaven," our Lord said, "over one sinner who repents." But that doesn't mean that the angels have to wait for sinners to do penance before they can have any joy or happiness. The angels and saints share in the joy of God when He is glorified by His creatures.

Purity of Intention and Worldly Success

Actually, working to please God, working for a pure intention, working not for ourselves but for the sake of God, results very often not only in peace but even worldly or material success as well. Wrong motives, on the other hand, seem at times to have a way of vitiating our powers and efforts. As Saint Thomas à Becket is made to say in the play, *Murder in the Cathedral,* "The last temptation is the greatest treason—to do the right thing for the wrong reason." Purifying our intention can often spell the difference between worldly success and failure.

Bearing cogent testimony to this thesis is a famous basketball player who had been an outstanding star not only in prep school but throughout his college career. However, during his senior year, his performance began to fall off badly. He would shoot and miss one basket after another. Everyone was asking what the matter was with him; but no one seemed to know, least of all he himself.

One day he was talking with one of the priests on the faculty at his university, trying to get at the root of his trouble. The priest questioned him about every conceivable factor, every possible angle of his problem. They tried to discover any circumstances existing at the time of his slump that were not existing previously.

Finally, the priest, in his probing, put his finger on something that seemed significant. In recent months, the basketball player had started to keep steady company with a girl friend. At the more recent games, she had been sitting in the crowd in Madison Square Garden. He admitted, at last, to the priest and to himself, that everytime he got his hands on the ball he was thinking of his girl friend up in the stands; he was putting on a show for her benefit, trying to make a basket to please her. Consequently, he was tense; he was pressing, trying too hard; he was not his old self.

The good priest recommended as a remedy that he try to purify his intention in playing basketball. Let his aim be to give glory to God through the use of his athletic talents and abilities rather than vainly to show off. "But, Father," he said, "in the midst of the bedlam in Madison Square Garden at a big basketball game, how can I have time to purify my intention, or how can I think to keep it pure?"

After much discussion of the point, they agreed that he would try this: Everytime he got his hands on the ball and was going to shoot for the basket, just as he would let the ball go he would say, "For Thee!" That was all. It would take only an instant. "For Thee!" That would be enough to purify his motive and to tell God that he was shooting that basket for Him and for His honor and glory.

Subsequent games proved that to be the remedy which enabled him to overcome his motive of pride for which he was working before, and which was destroying his basketball finesse. To achieve such worldly success, of course, is a poor motive for which to strive for purity of intention, but it does show how, if we are working to please God alone, we do not strain inordinately for results. Consequently, we achieve better results than if we were pressing or tense as a result of trusting in ourselves instead of in God.

However, the essential effect of purity of intention, or working to please God, in addition to glorifying Him and meriting for ourselves, is the peace that God intends us to have. It is that peace which results from right order, which comes from fulfilling the purpose of our existence by doing what we do to please and to glorify God.

How to Tell that Our Intention Is Pure

Since this is so, we might ask whether there are any ways by which we can know whether we have purity of intention. After all, it is very easy to deceive ourselves in this matter. We can say we are doing what we do for God, but are we, really? Is there any way we can tell for sure? Are there any signs by which we can confidently know that we're doing what we do to please God?

Actually, there are, and very infallible signs, too. We can tell whether we are working to please God alone by our attitude toward *what* we do, toward the *results* that we achieve, and toward the *rewards* or approval that we might get or not get from what we do.

Our Attitude to What We Do

First of all, our purity of intention can be gauged by our attitude to *what* we do, or what we are given to do. If we have purity of intention, if we are doing what we do to please God and not ourselves, then, obviously, we are indifferent to, and, in the final analysis, will have no preference for this work or that work or the other work that Almighty God gives us to do. We are content whether He gives us this duty or that duty or the other duty. We want only to be sure that God wants us to do this particular thing, and we can know that infallibly if it is part of the duties of our state in life, or if we have been assigned to it by superiors. Knowing that our task is God's will, we are deeply glad to do it with all our heart and strength. If we ask, "Why must I do that?" when told by superiors, we are far from simplicity and purity of intention.

Again, if our intention is truly pure, we put the very same effort into a fatiguing duty as we would into an easy duty; we put the same effort and enthusiasm and attention into an obscure, hidden, unglamorous duty as we would into an honorable duty, or one that would bring us praise and put us in the spotlight and cause admiration on the part of others. Or, if we had purity of intention, our enthusiasm for any work would not be measured by personal pleasure or personal satisfaction or reward.

While He was on this earth, our Divine Lord said, "My food is to do the will of him who sent me." He has made here a very significant choice of words. Food keeps us alive. We have to have food three time a day to be able to maintain ourselves. And what food is to our body, the will of the Father was to the Son. His meat was to do the will of the Father. That should be our meat also, no matter what position or duty we occupy. The meat of the Sister Portress, or the Brother Infirmarian, or the Sister in the habit room, or the Brother in the classroom, or in the ward of the hospital, is the same as the meat of the Superior General, the Provincial, or Novice Mistress, or Father-Rector, or anybody else in the community. The duty of each is the meat, the will of God for each of them. So, too, our duty, no matter what, should be our meat, should be the will of God for us. We should be as content in a lowly position as in a position of great responsibility.

The only important information we need is this: Is what we are about to do God's will? If it is, and we are doing it to please Him, then, it does not make any difference whether it is sweeping a floor, or giving a speech, or teaching a class. If we have purity of intention, we shall put the same effort and enthusiasm into each of them and glorify God as the angels do who veil their faces with their wings and sing, "Holy! Holy! Holy!"

If we go about the obscure, or the hard, or the unromantic, or unwanted tasks with reluctance, like a slave beaten to the burden, then we can be sure we are not working to please God; we are working to please ourselves. We can know this from the fact that since we do not happen to be pleased in this instance, we are not working particularly hard or with much enthusiasm. We are trying to get it done as quickly as we can, or leave as much of it undone as we can. So, there we have a test: How can we tell whether we are working to please ourselves or to please God? By our attitude to what we don't like to do, naturally speaking.

Another test of purity of intention is our attitude toward the *results* we achieve in what we do. If we are working to please God, then we are not upset if what we are doing does not turn out well. That is true whether we are sewing something, whether we are polishing a floor, whether we are sweeping, or teaching a class. If we have purity of intention, we are willing to accept God's will, even in failure. If we get all upset when what we do does not turn out well, recall that God is not upset. If we are working to please Him, then why are we upset?

Thank God that He does not judge us by results. He looks only at the effort we make with the knowledge we have, that is, the intention and motive we have in our mind and will. Are we so foolish as to think that God is dependent upon our puny efforts to achieve any success? Anything that we could do in a million years, God could do in an instant, in a million other and better ways. All He wants is our loving service, the efforts of our heart and soul to please Him. If we give Him that, there is no failure possible as long as we are doing His will, no matter what the material results of our work may be.

That is what we must be assured of. All God wants is our effort and our pure intention. "If thy eye be evil, thy whole body will be full of darkness." If our intention is wrong, then no matter what success we achieve, it is nothing in the eyes of God. On the other hand, no matter how a work may appear to fail, if we have done it with the right intention, to please God, then it is a success.

There is no possible worldly success, no potential material success that can give honor and glory to God like the service of our will, like doing His will to please Him. Did ever any work seem more a dismal failure than the work of Redemption? God's own Son came to earth and, after thirty years of preparation, He walked the highways and by-ways of the Holy Land curing and healing, and teaching the people, giving of Himself night and day, praying for them, doing penance for them. At the end of three years, rejected by all but a few who could be counted on the fingers of one hand, He died spiked to a post like a common criminal between two other criminals. Did ever anything look more like a failure than that? Yet, at the end of it, He could cry out in a voice of triumph the cry, not of a failure, but of a success: "It is consummated!" What is finished? "The work Thou hast given me to do." *That* is success! However much it might have looked like failure in the eyes of the world, it was the greatest success ever achieved or ever to be achieved.

So it is with our puny efforts and with the works that we have to do. It is not how we succeed that matters, but how we try to do what God wants us to do to please Him. It is not how much we do of what we want to do that counts with God, but how well we try to do what He wants us to do. So, then, we know we have purity of intention if we are concerned only with doing as best we can whatever God gives us to do, leaving the results to Him, whether they be success or failure. If we have purity of intention, we accept all with equanimity, with a peaceful mind, knowing that God is glorified not by what we do, but by our intentions and the efforts with which we do what He gives us to do.

On the other hand, if we get all upset when things do not turn out well, when things that we do turn out not so glowingly, if we are upset at that, it is because our motive, our intention was to achieve personal success. Then, when we do not, we are disappointed and we are sad. That is a sure indication that our intention was not pure, that we were not working for God.

Thus, we can tell if we are working for God with a pure intention by our attitude toward the results that we achieve in our work, by our attitude toward failure and success. If the thing that we do turns out successfully we should thank God for it, and give the glory to Him. "Do not rejoice in this," said our Lord when the apostles came back boasting that they were able to cast out devils. He had given them that power and they went out and tried it and it worked, and they came back saying excitedly, "We were casting out devils!" He responded, "Do not rejoice in this . . . but rejoice in this, that your names are written in heaven." That is the only thing in which to rejoice, not the puny little worldly successes that we might achieve, the tiny, futile, material honors we might amass. Do not rejoice in these, but that your name is written in Heaven. In the same way, we should rejoice with God if what we do truns out unsuccessfully. If we have done it for Him, He has been glorified. It matters not that we be not glorified for our lack of success. "He must increase, but I must decrease."

Our Attitude to Others' Success

Another test of our purity of intention, or manifestation of it, is our ability to rejoice at the success of *others* without being jealous of them, without being envious of them. If we have in mind only the good pleasure of God, we shall be glad at their success in their school work, in their community work, in their apparent success in the practice of virtue and the overcoming of their faults. On the other hand, if we are uneasy at their success, if we feel envious of it, if we wish they were not so successful, that is a sign that we are not seeking the glory of God; it is a sign that we have in mind, subconsciously at least, to come out on top, and that we are working for our own glory instead of God's. Because they seem to be threatening our position, we are uneasy at it, or we are jealous of it, or we are envious of their success.

If we have purity of intention, we would react like Moses did to others' success. Someone came to him complaining that another was prophesying, and Moses said, "O that all the people might prophesy . . . !" In effect he was saying, "Would that God would give it to everyone to glorify Him by prophesying as He has given me to be able to glorify Him." So, too, if we have purity of intention, if we are working to please God, we shall be glad when He is glorified by anybody, even by those we like the least.

Our Attitude to the Reward We Get

It is clear that we can test our purity of intention in these ways: By our attitude to *what* we have to do, whether it is to our liking or not; by our attitude toward the *results* we achieve, whether they are successful or not; finally, we can test the purity of our intention by our attitude toward the *reward* or thanks we receive for what we do. If we are working to please God and not ourselves, we are indifferent to praise or blame on the part of men. If, after doing a piece of work, we are sad or upset because we do not get superiors' notice, because they do not praise us for it, or because they do not tell us how wonderful we are, that is a sign that we were not working for God but for the reward or for that notice. We can tell this is so, for why else are we sad when we haven't received it.

If we are working for God, if we truly have purity of intention, we do what God wants us to do in the best way we can, even if nobody sees it, even if nobody says a word about it. After all, why should superiors thank us for doing our duty when we are not working for them? We are working for God, and He does not have a habit of stepping down to earth physically every once in a while and patting us on the back and saying, "That's wonderful work, Sister, keep it up!" But while He does not do that tangibly, we do know that He is grateful. We know this by faith, and that same faith should motivate us to be pure in our intention of working to please God alone.

The same purity of intention makes us indifferent to that diabolical evil, human respect, by which we so often do what we do so that people will think well of us; or we avoid what we should do because people will think ill of us. If we act only to please God, we will destroy this demon of human respect which causes, very often, so much damage in the novitiate and at the beginning of religious life.

Purity of Intention and Manifesting Our Faults

It is this same human respect, for example, that keeps us from discussing our external faults and failings in communication with our director or novice-mistress. We know such manifestation of ourselves is God's will. This is the task that God has given us to do as a means to our spiritual formation and growth, especially in the novitiate. This is the "what" that He would have us do, and if we live with purity of intention, we will do it. Should it be a fact that we will not do it, it indicates that to that extent at least, we are not pure in our intention. It is a proof that we are trying to please ourselves, that we want to maintain what we falsely think is our virtuous reputation in the mind of superiors or directors. Actually, if we only realized it, they would think much more of us for manifesting ourselves quite simply, because, since they think much more of virtue than they do of vice, they consequently think much more of humility than they do of pride. It is only pride that would prevent us from doing our duty, from seeking the guidance we need to grow in the perfection that we came to religious life to achieve.

Sometimes novices in particular have the erroneous notion that if they tell their faults against the rule or customs of community life, superiors will send them home. How foolish! Superiors are not in office to get rid of novices;

they are there to help them, and to form them spiritually
and religiously. This arrangement is predicated on the
obvious assumption that novices *need* forming. It is pre-
sumed that they do not come to the novitiate as perfect
Religious. Otherwise, superiors would not be wasting community money and time conducting a novitiate.

But superiors will be unable to help us unless we, as
novices, want to be helped; unless we are willing to cooperate and admit our shortcomings and faults. Thus the first
step in achieving that result is to overcome human respect,
the shame that the devil puts in us which prevents our
having the humility to discuss our failings for the purpose
of getting help. Such a spirit of humility and simplicity
is, of course, necessary not only while we are novices. It
will also be equally necessary all the days of our religious
life if we are sincerely striving for holiness, for it is an
indispensable means to religious perfection.

The day of profession is sacred in the memory of every
Religious. But if, on that day, the innermost thoughts of
each could be revealed, it is probable that everyone of them
would be tinged with pangs of regret for not having made
better use of the time in the novitiate. And high on any
list of causes for lost or regretted time in the novitiate must
be written the vice of human respect and lack of purity
of intention.

Purity of Intention and Formation Time

If all the members of any community could pass one
by one in a parade, so to speak, before their novices, and
pause for a moment to speak what they regarded as important advice for those in a novitiate, no doubt all would
say in some manner: "Don't waste your precious time of
novitiate; don't wait three, six, or nine months before you
find out what it is all about. Strive so as never to have

any regrets when your novitiate is over, because of human respect. Don't fail in observance because, perhaps, you might feel foolish or embarrassed, or do not see the wisdom of certain customs; or because you do not recognize the importance of silence or recollection, or trying to get the spirit of the novitiate from the very start; do not kick against the goad because you cannot see the prudence or the sense in certain humiliations and penitential practices that you must do; or because you cannot see the virtue in adopting all the little customs they have in the novitiate, especially the customs that nobody sees you observe."

Each of those returning Religious would tell the novices: "Observe them all! Get the spirit from the very beginning because, before you get very many years older, you will see the value of them all. You will see, over and above their intrinsic value, their tremendous part in the shaping of your spiritual life. You will see their worth in the practice they give you in bending your own will to the will of God; for every one of those customs and practices is God's will for you. Observe them not because you see *why*, or not because you see the wisdom of them, but because you know with the certainty of faith they are what God wants you to do."

Each of those visiting members of the community would go on to point out that all the rules and practices the novices are trying to keep have been observed by every Religious of the community from the very beginning, from the Superior General down through all the provincial and local superiors, and all the private Religious throughout the whole world. They have been observed by them all and they must be observed by us if we would please God.

If we had purity of intention, we would not be concerned with whether the one next to us keeps them, whether she thinks they are foolish or not, whether she can see the wisdom of them or not. Our companion is not going to be with us when we stand before the judgement seat of God to answer for the graces of our vocation. We are going to be stark alone at that instant. If we have striven to please Him now by purity of intention in our actions, we have the consolation of knowing that we shall please Him then.

After the great Saint Bernard died, they found among his papers writings to this effect: "I have not come here to the monastery to live as others live, but as they ought to live. And so, when I came, I was given a rule to follow and not the lives of others; I was not told to do what the others do, but I was told to live by this rule and therefore I must keep all of the rules, even if nobody else keeps one of them." Such was Saint Bernard and his attitude to the rules and customs of his community. Such also is the purity of intention that we should resolve to have right from the very beginning of our community life.

A story is told of some visitors being shown through a famous monastery. An ancient monk in a soiled habit was working in the kitchen. So venerable looking was he that one of the visitors asked him how long he had been in the community. His reply was: "Oh, I don't know; not a day, perhaps." His questioners appeared so very puzzled and surprised that he said, "Oh, I have worn this habit for sixty-five years; but if we compute time by my works and the purity of intention with which I have done them, I do not know how long I have been a Religious."

How long have we been in the novitiate, or in the community? Let us not measure time in weeks, or months, or years that we have worn our holy habit, but in the weeks and years we have lived well and have worked with purity of intention. How many are there in our life?

From the earliest days of our religious life we should determine not to waste time in the novitiate, merely going through the external motions. Such a course appears all the more tragic when we realize that the happiness that we get out of the novitiate, or out of religious life, is in direct pro-

portion to the effort that we put into it. If we are ever unhappy in the community, if we ever have one unhappy day
in the novitiate or on the missions, we should look immediately to the source of the trouble and ask ourselves, "How
much effort have I put into living the life of the novitiate
or the community? How much effort am I putting into acquiring its spirit? How much am I giving every bit of me
in living the spirit of my vocation?"

We cannot find true peace unless we are giving one hundred percent. It is foolish to pretend that we can be happy
out of our element which we are in religion if we are not trying to live it to the full. We cannot be happy in that way
any more than a fish can be happy out of water. Let no
novice in the religious life ever say, "It was six months or
nine months before I even found out what it was all about
and really began to try." If we do not know what it is all
about, ask. God has placed His representatives there to tell
us.

Purity of Intention and Feelings

Our sole aim, then, should be to please God in keeping
our rule, in our studies, in our spiritual exercises, in our duties, in our serving, in whatever it may be that we do. "Do
all for the glory and honor of God." But mark this well:
Inevitably there must be times when we won't *feel* like being
indifferent to what we have to do, or the results that we
achieve, or the reward, whether praise or blame. Very
likely, most of the time we won't feel like being indifferent
to the manifestation of our faults; or we won't *feel* like making the effort necessary to acquire the spirit of the novitiate
or community, and so on. But feelings, let it be repeated,
have nothing to do with holiness. They have no moral-
ity. Actually, the less we feel like doing what we have to
do, the more merit there will be in doing it, the more does

it show our love for God. For doing something when we do
not feel like it shows we are not doing it to please ourselves,
and thus we can be sure we are doing it for Him if we have
made that intention.

The surest means to acquire such purity of intention and,
actually, the test of our purity of intention, is to say, "Thanks
God," in distasteful situations. To thank God and ask Him
for His helping grace when we do not like what we have to
do, or when we don't like the way we are asked to do it, or
do not like the results we achieve, to grit our teeth and say,
"Thanks, God, this is for you," and do it—*all that* is purity of
intention in action!

At such times, we are like our Lord in the Garden. He
hated so what He had to do that He prayed that He would
not have to do it: "Father, if thou wilt, remove this chalice
from me; but yet not my will, but thine be done." He was
saying in effect, "Thanks, God, this is what You want, I
will do it." So, in imitation of Him, we should strive to develop the habit of saying, "Thanks, God," when we have to
do something that we don't like. Let us pray thus: "There
is no satisfaction in this for me, but I will do it for You dear
God."

But our aim should be higher yet. We should strive not
only to begin with that intention, but we should also renew
it just as often as we can during our actions. We should
renew it especially as often as we are tempted to rebel in
the midst of doing something we don't like; just as often as
we are tempted to resent the results that we achieve, or be
upset at our failure; just as often as we are tempted to feel
sad because we do not get praise. To thank God when we
do not succeed, to thank God for what we don't like, is the
surest sign that we are working to please Him and that we
have purity of intention. Having that, we have an added
consolation. If we can thank God in the midst of things we

don't like to do, thus showing that we have purity of intention, then we can be sure that we shall also have purity of intention and be working to please Him in the things we like to do.

CHAPTER XIII

Humility

HUMILITY IS ONE of the two virtues that our Divine Lord asked us specifically and expressly to learn of Him. "Learn from me," he said, "for I am meek and humble of heart." Humility was the unifying principle of the whole life of our Divine Lord, and it is one of the foundation stones of our spiritual life. Hence, the importance of having clear notions of this virtue.

Many difficulties arise in the practice of humility because of false concepts of the true nature of humility. Very often the virtue of humility is thought of as certain external acts which *seem* humble or which we hope will be interpreted by others as being humble. In the popular mind, it signifies a kind of "Uriah Heep" hand-wringing self-depreciation, which could not possibly be meant by anyone in his right mind.

Saint Bernard tells us that there are three kinds of humble people, and two of them are not humble. First there are those who *feel* humble; they feel lowdown. Perhaps they are victims of an inferiority complex. They are like the man who said he felt so low he could reach up and touch bottom. But Saint Bernard tells us that because we feel low or feel humble doesn't mean that we are humble.

Secondly there are those who think they are humble. They like to think speculatively about how humble they are and how unworthy they are. They exaggerate their own faults so others will get the impression that such insignificant failures could not possibly be real faults and hence their exaggeration must be due to humility. But Saint Bernard says that because they think speculatively that they are humble doesn't mean that they are humble; they only think they are.

The true virtue of humility is not a matter of external acts. It is essentially an internal habit of the soul which inclines us to act in a certain way. It is a virtue which disposes us to realize our true position before God, and to *act* in accord with that reality. In other words, humility is based on a realization of what we truly are in God's sight and demands that we act in accordance with that realization.

Our True Position Before God

Humility is a volitional virtue which moderates our desire for excellence. Sometimes it is said that humility is truth, but more properly speaking, it perfects our *will* and has to do not so much with knowing the truth as with loving and seeking the good. However, it is based on the truth of what we really are in God's sight. And what is our position in the sight of God?

Actually, God made us out of nothing. We are absolutely nothing of ourselves. We had nothing to do with our coming into being; we can have nothing to do with our going out of existence. True, we can commit suicide and thus have something to do with going out of this worldly existence; but our *true* existence is eternal and is lived either in heaven or hell. We are absolutely and completely dependent upon Almighty God, not only for our existence, but for every single thing that is needed for or flows from that existence; for everything that we have, every gift, every

talent, every ability, the very breath we breathe we are dependent on Him. We can do nothing of ourselves. "What
hast thou that thou hast not received?" asks Saint Paul.
"And if thou hast received it, why dost thou boast as if thou
hadst not received it?" "Without me you can do nothing,"
says our Divine Lord.

A Further Essential Detail

But this complete helplessness and insufficiency does not
yet present the entire true picture of us. There is more. In
addition to depending absolutely on Almighty God for every
gift we have, including the major gift of existence, we have
abused and mis-used his gifts and become worthy of punishment. Therefore, not only are we not accountable for anything good that we have; but we have, by sin, *forfeited our
right* to anything good we have. By sin we have merited
any evil that could possibly befall us as a punishment of sin.

What is our true position before God? Perhaps an example
will help us realize it. A television program called *Candid
Camera* used to conceal sound motion picture cameras and
take movies of people unknown to them. Later, amid great
consternation, the secret would be revealed to them. Recalling that example is a good device for helping us realize
what we are truly before God and what we are in our own
conscience.

Imagine that a candid motion picture sound camera had
been secretly training on us at every moment of our lives
since the very dawn of reason. Suppose that, unknown to
us, a complete sound motion picture film of our life had been
made by that camera. Following us like our shadow, it had
been grinding away each moment of our life, every morning, noon, and night, every hour, every minute of our childhood, youth, and till now. Then imagine that in our
community room or recreation room our movie was going to

be run off for all our companions, our own life story, complete, as it really was night and day, alone, with others. The audio-visual record on that film is what we are before God. *That* is our true position before God. Humility means that we shape our conduct according to that truth.

Therefore, humility is the disposition of will to restrain the tendency in all of us to claim esteem beyond that which is our due. If we are humble, there will be no posing, no pretense, no attempts to appear better than we really are, to be something that we really are not. Humility implies all that, and more!

The reason we can be humiliated is that we have not developed the habit of acting according to the rule of humility. Suppose, for example, on coming down out of the pulpit in the refectory, before all the community, we fell flat on our face. We can imagine our embarrassment and humiliation. Why are we humiliated in such a situation? The reason is we are not humble; it is because we feel we are in a position which is somehow beneath our dignity. "I'm certainly not so stupid as to fall down coming out of this pulpit, and I can't bear having all these people thinking I am that stupid."

We are thus humiliated because we like to put on a show; we like to put up a front; we like to appear brighter, smarter, more alert than we are. We like to present a revised and expurgated version of that life movie of ours for the general public. The one that is known only to God and us must be safely hidden and guarded in the storage vaults or archives of our own conscience, because we must never appear as we truly are! Such a conviction, such an attitude is the antithesis of humility.

Above all, if we are acting in accord with the truth of our true position before God, if we are humble, we submit to God's will for us, particularly when that will is unpleasant or untoward. We accept graciously criticism, unkindnesses, injustices, all the other hardships we have to bear from others. It was in this that our Divine Saviour most clearly manifested His humility which He proposed to us as a model.

The Humility of Christ

But if we would understand the unbelievable extent of the humility of our Divine Lord, we must go in spirit back far beyond His public life, to the Incarnation, to the very moment of the Annunciation, for there is where His humility began to appear.

To get some faint idea of the completeness with which God emptied Himself, as Saint Paul tells us He did, we would have to resort to an outlandish comparison. Yet this comparison is not so inconceivable that God Himself did not seize upon the very same metaphor to describe His humiliation in the Passion. Through the lips of his psalmist, He said of Himself, "I am a worm and no man."

With that prophecy as a cue, we can imagine a fabulous situation in which a man, for some good, justifiable reason would be able to and would want to become a worm, actually a worm, for the sake of worms, and for some good he could do for them. While still retaining his human nature, that is, his intellect and will, he would take on himself the form of a worm and be confined in his movements to the ground. He would submit to the condition of a worm and be driven up out of the ground in a sudden rain, lest he drown; suffering all the indignities to which worms are subject: being threaded on a fish hook, being eaten by robins, and so on. Such a lowering of himself by a human being is unthinkable, even if it were possible to some man.

Yet the difference between a man's nature and the nature of a worm, while tremendous, is still measurable; but the difference between Almighty God, the Eternal Creator, and the nature of man that He made out of nothing, is *infinite*. His taking on the nature of man is infinitely more degrading, if you will, than would be a man's taking on the nature of a worm. Saint Paul tells of it in the only way he could say it: "He *emptied* himself, taking the nature of a slave and being made like unto men. And appearing in the form of man, he humbled himself, becoming obedient to death, even to the death on a cross."

To continue the fantastic analogy, we would think that even if a man were inconceivably to take upon himself the form of a worm for some reason, he would at least select a place for himself among the better class of worms, if there be such a thing. One would think he would choose to be a ruler of some kind. We would think that if he took upon himself the nature of a worm, he would be in some position of esteem or influence. Yet, when Christ became a man, He was born in an obscure corner of the world of the obscure laboring class. He was no prince; he was no ruler. Born of humble parents, He was put to death at the end like a criminal.

Now if we could *realize* that fact, then we would have some notion of how God really humbled Himself in becoming man in the first place. While still remaining God, with His infinite knowledge, power, and goodness, He confined Himself to man's way of acting and thinking, and walking, and so on. All the time that He was on earth, perfectly and infinitely holy in Himself, He chose deliberately for Himself all the consequences of life which He would have deserved as punishment had He been the worst of sinners like ourselves. Of His own will, He took upon himself all the punishments due to sin.

This was the proof and the manifestation of the humility of Christ; not His humble condition or the poverty of His life. A person can be in lowly position and be poor without being humble at all. The humility of Christ was the internal disposition of His will to accept all the contradiction and suffering that He would have deserved had He been a sinner in truth, as we are. He submitted uncomplainingly to all the trials and tribulations and crosses of this life that flow from the malice of sin. That was His humility of action.

Humility and Punishment for Sin

But we are actual sinners. Everyone of us has sinned personally. Because we have sinned, we deserve to suffer in punishment thereof. Therefore, our humility will manifest itself in the disposition of will to accept what we have to suffer in this life as justly due to us because of our true position of sinners before God. If we rebel at the slings and arrows of outrageous fortune, if we complain at contradictions, misunderstandings, corrections, adversities, trials, sicknesses, troubles, problems it is because we are not humble. It is because we are not regulating our conduct in accord with that true picture of ourselves as we are before God.

If we ever committed one tiny sin, the least venial sin, no punishment on earth can fully make amends for it. God revealed this to Saint Catherine. To offend the infinite God who has made us out of nothing for Himself, who sustains us in being with no desserts or rights of our own, is to reach up and bite the hand that holds us over the abyss of nothingness; it is to commit the worst kind of treason. If we have done that but once, nothing we can suffer on this earth can adequately atone for it. We deserve more than we can ever suffer in this life, either in intensity or in duration.

But so often we rebel at what we have to suffer from others. How different is our conduct from the example of the Divine Lord who resented nothing, crosses, trials, contradictions, denials, slights, ingratitude, persecution, suffering, even a cruel death. He did not use His divine power to escape one bit of it, to alleviate it one iota. He was humble! He accepted all in our stead; He accepted the cross as we should accept it; He accepted and suffered all that He suffered as if He were deserving of it all, as we in fact and in truth are.

The necessity of living in the midst of opposition, contradiction, trial, suffering is a consequence of sin, original sin and our own. Being humble means accepting all these things without bitterness, without resentment, without complaint, without impatience. It means we bow gracefully to them because we deserve much more. It means we accept all crosses with patience.

When we are impatient, we are rebelling against the will of God; we are resenting what God sends us; we are telling God that He has no right to give us this punishment because we do not deserve it. The truth is, of course, we deserve infinitely more. Thus, if we are humble, we recognize that we merit any suffering that comes to us, and that nothing we can suffer on this earth can ever fully repair the damage we have done or the offense that we have given to God by our deliberate sin.

The Positive Side of Humility

But, in addition to accepting as our just due whatever evil might befall us, there is a positive aspect to this virtue, the practice of which is often overlooked or misunderstood. Humility is based on truth. But the truth on which it is based is *one*. Therefore, real and valid humility must be based on or flow from the whole truth. And the whole truth about anyone is that God has given that one undeniable gifts and endowments and talents, both of nature and of grace.

Humility, then, does not mean self-depreciation. Being humble does not mean that we must deny the endowments of nature or grace that Almighty God has given us. If God has given someone a magnificent voice, it is not humble for her to pretend that she sings like a frog, or to deny in any way the gift that God has given her. Humility, to repeat, is based on truth, and the truth is that God *has* given her a truly beautiful voice. Therefore, she should not deny it, but attribute it to God, which is positive humility.

Our Divine Lord Himself, infinite perfection, said to His followers: "Learn from me for I am meek and humble of heart." But He also said to His enemies, "Which of you can convict me of sin?" Thereby He proclaimed His unique sinlessness. Our Blessed Mother did not deny the wonderful prerogatives Almighty God had lavished on her. "Because He who is mighty has done great things for me," she sang, "all generations shall call me blessed." Is this the Virgin most humble? "All generations shall call me blessed!" Surely! That future, perpetual benediction was a gift that Almighty God had given her, "because He has regarded the lowliness of his handmaid." But note what she says: "He that is mighty has done great things for me." She claimed no applause for her greatness; she put the credit for her gifts where it belonged, namely, with God.

Saint Paul calls himself, "the least of the apostles." That is what he was of himself. But he also says, "But, by the grace of God, I am what I am, and his grace in me has not been fruitless—in fact I have labored more than any of them." Saint Paul was saying in effect, "I have labored more abundantly than Peter, the first Pope, the one whom Christ made the head of his Church; more abundantly than James and John, who went up on the mountain with Him; more abundant than Philip and all the others. I, Paul, have labored more abundantly than all of them." Talk about boasting! No! Not at all, for he explains, "Yet not I, but the grace of God with me." He gave the credit where credit was due. Similarly, Saint Thomas Aquinas claimed to have the gift of never reading anything which he did not understand completely and remember always; but he did not attribute this gift to himself, he attributed it to God where it belonged.

The difference between our Blessed Mother, Saint Paul, Saint Thomas, and all humble ones, and ourselves is that they attribute their gifts and prerogatives to their proper source which is Almighty God our Father. On the other hand, we so often childishly attribute our gifts and accomplishments to ourselves. "See my medals! Am I not grand!" How foolish can we become! We are like a man driving an armored express truck transferring gold and securities from one bank to another. Wouldn't he be foolish to drive by his girl friend's house and pretend that all the gold in his truck was his own? It is no more his than it is the bank president's. Therefore, would he not be foolish to pretend because he was driving a truck full of gold that he was better than the man driving the ash truck for the city? Very likely the ash truck driver gets a much bigger paycheck at the end of the week than the bank truck driver, even though he has been carrying around with him throughout the week a much less enviable load.

It will be the same in heaven. Persons with few gifts, with meager talent, or looks, or abilities, or achievement may get the much greater reward because of the humble way they did their work for God with what they had, than the persons with all the talents, and all looks, and all the ability, but who attributed their gifts to themselves so foolishly, and sought and basked in their own glory.

Therefore, humility does not at all mean denying the gifts, and the abilities, and the talent, and attributes which Almighty God has given us; but it does mean that we attribute them not to ourselves but to God. It demands that we use them, not for our own display, not for getting the praise of others, but to be useful to ourselves and others and thereby give glory to God. If we are humble, we use our gifts of nature and grace to do good; we use them to spread God's kingdom, His glory. We follow the counsel of our Divine Lord: "Let your light shine before men, in order that they may see your good works and give glory to your Father in heaven." Let your light shine before men, He tells us.

That is, do not hide it under a bushel; do not conceal the talents and abilities that we have. Use them; but use them for the glory of God.

If, as a result of our doing this, others praise us, let us refer the praise to God instead of proudly soaking it up ourselves. We can say in reply to a compliment: "Well, God is good." Or, if we are tempted to feel proud over anything God has given us or done through us, we should strive to develop the habit of praying to ourselves. "Not to us, O Lord, not to us, but to thy name give glory," as the Psalmist said. To attribute what we have to God, where the credit belongs; to say, "God is good," when we are praised; to use our talents and abilities not for our own glory but for the glory of God; all this is the positive practice of humility.

Humility in Failures and Speech

Humility can also be manifested, and in fact must be manifested even in failure. Very often, in community life, we are asked to do something for which we feel we do not have the ability, or the time, or the acumen to do a first-rate job. So, we try to get out of it. But that is not humility. If we are asked to do something by legitimate superiors, it is God asking us to do it. If we feel incompetent, we are permitted to represent our reasons. But if, in spite of that, we are still asked to do it, we should do the best we can with what we have in the way of talent, ability, or material. Having done our best, God looks for nothing else and He is glorified by our effort and intention alone.

God does not judge us by the results we produce but by our efforts and intention. Even if our project does not turn out well, even if it is an outright failure, that failure is God's will and it is a lot better for us than success in that instance. If we fail at any time, God keeps us humble thereby, and that is what counts in the ultimate analysis; whereas, if we succeed, we might give way to pride, and that would be worse than any material failure could possibly be. Humility, then, has a great place in our attitude toward and ability to cope with failure, that failure with which we are all inevitably faced at one time or another.

It is also manifested in our conversation by letting others choose the subject, and by speaking little of ourselves. We must not be one of those who have a very clever and ingenious way of swinging every topic and every subject around to some situation or some slant in which they can take the conversational ball and carry it for a long period of time. They maneuver the trend of conversation so that they can dominate the group with the story of their exploits, of what they have done, of what they can do. This, in spite of the fact that if they had studied the slightest bit of anatomy, they could tell by the way their arms are hung that they were not made to pat themselves on the back. "What hast thou that thou hast not received? And if thou hast received it, why dost thou boast as if thou hadst not received it?" What have we done that God has not given us the wherewithal to do it; and if we have received the wherewithal to do what we do, why do we glory as if we have not received it?

Humility and Unsought Humiliations

Again, the practice of humility is demanded, perhaps most frequently, in the acceptance of little humiliations which come to us unlooked for, the kind of humiliations we do not seek, but which Almighty God sends us directly. They are the best sort of humiliations for which to be alert. When others express contempt for us, when our talents are overlooked, when we receive bad treatment, when others are chosen to do something that we would like to do—or that we feel we could do better than the ones chosen—or when we receive corrections and advices, these are all God-given opportunities to practice humility by accepting them graciously.

On the other hand, to accuse and excuse is a mark of pride; to accuse others for mistakes we make and excuse ourselves is the mark of a proud person. How easy it is to say in self-defense: "The reason that turned out that way was because Sister so and so said such and such." Or, "Brother so and so did such and such." Or, "I was going to do it that way but Sister said not to." We blame everybody else, accuse everybody for our failures and faults, and excuse ourself. Doing so proclaims our pride!

But the humble are ever ready to accuse themselves. Recall the Pharisee and the Publican. Hear the Pharisee accusing the poor publican: "I thank you God, that I am not like the rest of men . . . or even like this publican." But the poor publican did not accuse anybody but himself. He didn't even think to excuse himself: "O God, be merciful to me the sinner." But our Lord said that he went down to his house justified rather than the other.

Humility in the Novitiate

In speaking of the importance of humility, it should be pointed out that it is an indispensable virtue, particularly at the beginning of religious life in the novitiate. The novitiate is a time of formation. A time of formation involves forming; and forming will necessarily involve trial and error, and correction for errors. Therefore, in community life, we might as well face it, we are going to be corrected. However, it is possible for somebody who is immature and a little childish to go all to pieces because she is corrected. Maybe she goes off into a corner and cries and tells herself: "I am a failure." Then she becomes sad and resentful because Sister corrected her, because she told her she did this or that wrong, or that she must do it another way the next time.

But acting thus is far from humility. If we were truly humble, we would realize that we most probably deserve correction when we get it. Think of all the times we were deserving of correction and did not get it. Therefore even an undeserved correction helps pay off an unpaid debt of reparation. So humility demands that we do not have such a strange and distorted view of our own excellency that we think we are never in any way deserving of correction. If we are corrected and have humility, we don't get all broken up about the correction, and cry and feel sad and resentful.

Humility is based on truth, and the truth is that those who correct us are simply doing their duty. They are doing what we, in fact, asked them to do when we came to the community. When we entered, we asked: "Will you show me how to be perfect? Will you guide me and form me into a truly spiritual person?" Since we asked the community to do that, humility demands that we do not resent it when they fulfill our request and do it for us.

Three Attitudes Toward Humiliations

Actually, there are several attitudes we can take toward humiliations which come to us unsought. We can rebel against them; or we can merely accept them; or we can accept them cheerfully or even go looking for them. If we rebel against them, it is bad, because then we are rebelling against the will of God; we're rebelling against what God is sending us and what God wills to happen to us. Thus, we must struggle not to rebel against humiliations. We must at least accept them, that is, *put up with them,* take them without rebelling. If we do, it is good. We then have the least common denominator of a manifestation of the virtue of humility, namely, to accept humiliations without resentment and without rebellion.

Those who are better, the more advanced in the spiritual

life, not only accept humiliations, but they accept them *cheerfully,* because they thereby imitate our Divine Lord more closely. They are more like our Lord on the cross. They accept humiliations cheerfully, because thus they can participate more fully in His apostolate of salvation for the world; thus they can share more actively in His redemptive work.

The good, then, put up with or accept humiliation; the better, the more advanced, are cheerful in the face of humiliations. Finally, the best, the saints, go looking for humiliations. They seek out contradictions because they love the cross of Christ so much they want to seek it, rather than wait for it to come, so that more and more they may be co-re-deemers with Christ.

But, at very least, we must strive to be *good,* that is, to accept and put up with the humiliations we meet day by day. If, in our pride, we rebel against them, we are telling God that we don't deserve what He is sending us. But that is not the truth and, therefore, we are not humble.

Admittedly, it is a long, hard road to acquire facility in the virtue of humility. But it is a goal that will never be reached unless we start. Furthermore, there is no time like the present to begin to acquire this facility. If we ever think that we have reached it, and that we can rest on our oars, just recall this fact: if we can be humiliated, we still are not humble.

CHAPTER XIV

The Blessed Virgin and Our Spiritual Exercises

IT IS EMPHASIZING the obvious to say that our Blessed Lady loves all men. After the love which God bears for mankind, there is no greater love possible than the love which Mary has for all men. So great is her love that she willed to become the co-redeemer of mankind by sharing in the Passion of Christ in a way and to an extent that no one ever did.

But if our Blessed Lady has this tremendous love for all men, even sinners, for a greater reason does she have a consuming love for those in religious life, for those who have given their lives to her Son. What must be her love for those who lead a life which involves frequent meditation on the Mother of God, on her life, and on her virtues? How she must love those who celebrate her feast so faithfully, and who so often turn to her to pray for help. Who can estimate the love that she must have for such as these? The Church accommodates to Mary the words of sacred scripture: "They that work by me shall not sin. They that explain me shall have life everlasting." This gives us an inkling of the reward that we can expect from a life as closely associated with our Blessed Lady, and as concerned with devotion to our Blessed Lady as that of the religious life.

Mary and Our Vocation

We know, of course, that all the interminable series of actual graces that have come to us and have resulted in the realization of our vocation have come to us through the hands of our Blessed Lady herself. Therefore, we owe a special debt of gratitude to Mary because of this fact. We owe her thanks for her part in our being called to a life in which we have so many reminders of her, so many more reminders of her than we would have had in the world. She is called to our mind in our morning prayers, in the Angelus three times a day; in our evening prayers, by her statues about our houses, in our rosary at our side, and in so many other ways. We have the great privilege of being called to a life in which we are constantly made aware of our Blessed Lady.

Because she has been instrumental in obtaining the graces of our vocation for us, and because she has worked with us even when we did not realize it, kneading and softening our hearts and making them pliable and receptive to God's grace leading to our consecration to Him; because she has been the channel and the instrument through which we have received those graces, therefore she is vitally interested in the conduct and outcome of our vocation. She not only can help us, but she also *wants* to help us.

Virgin Most Powerful

She can help us in all the difficulties and trials of our vocation, because she is *Virgo Potens*, Virgin Most Powerful. Tradition has honored Mary with the title, *Omnipotentia supplex*, omnipotence in the order of supplication. This is so because, first of all, she is loved by God more than any creature He ever made. God, in turn, we are told by theologians, is loved by her more than by all creatures put together. Secondly, over and above that bond of mutual love that exists between them as Creator and creature, she was also the mother of God. Therefore, her slightest wish with God takes on the nature of a maternal command. God, who is her dutiful Son, is anxious to please His mother.

Thus, she is the one who is able to help us in our vocation; she is the one to whom we should turn in the trials of our vocation, because she, after God, has the most sincere interest in it. As a matter of fact, she is more vitally interested in it than we are ourselves. Did she not stand on a hot hillside and was she not crowned queen of martyrs to help merit the grace of our vocation? So, if our Blessed Lady loves all mankind, she has a very special love for us in religious life.

Now, if Mary has any way in which she would want us to show our appreciation of her love for us, it would be that we model our lives on hers; that we become ever more conscious of her; that we keep her with us and make our lives increasingly more like hers.

Mary's Life and Its Value

Her whole life could be summed up in a few words of her Magnificat: "My soul magnifies the Lord." She lived to glorify God. Her life was a life of union with God, of love for His glory, and zeal to do His will. She was consumed not only with union with God, but also by union with Christ, her Son. But the whole purpose and end of the life of Christ was to make His Father known, loved, and glorified. At the end of His life, at the last supper, He said, "I have glorified thee on earth . . . and now do thou, Father, glorify me." Thus, just as our Lord lived to glorify the Father and lead others to do so, Mary also lived for the same reason. Mary and her Son, Christ, were one in glorifying the Father, in living for His glory.

Our lives as Religious are also for that same purpose, namely, to continue and carry on the work of our Blessed Lady and of her Divine Son, the work of living for God, glorifying the Father by living with our wills united to His will. We are chosen to carry out the very work that Mary and Christ did when they were on earth.

But what did Mary do to glorify God? Did she found a religious community? Did she perform rigorous and extraordinary penances? Do we read of anything that our Blessed Lady did that we could not do? She washed the clothes, and fed her child, and swept the house and took care of it; she went to a wedding feast; she walked across the Jordan and about Judea. What did she do? She did nothing that we cannot do.

But what made Mary's work so valuable for glorifying God and meriting grace was the *intention* with which she did it. Whatever she did was done because it was what God wanted her to do at that moment. She did not complain; she did not rebel because she was not located in a more pleasant or more prominent city, or because she did not have a prestige duty. She was not in the foreground at any time during all the public life of her Son; she was in the background; she was hidden. She came to the foreground only when it was time to undergo suffering and martyrdom on Calvary. Otherwise, she did nothing that we do not do every day of our lives. Yet, what she did glorified God like the work of no creature before or since because of the love with which she did it, because of the union of her will with God's will. Her every smallest deed glorified God because she did *what* God wanted, *when* He wanted it, in the *best way* she could to *please Him.* To this also we are called as Religious and consecrated souls, namely, to live continually to give glory to God, to live with our wills united to the will of God.

He sees to it that we have the means to do this at every moment. In calling us to the community, He guarantees to furnish the means to achieve our goal. He gives us daily Mass and Communion, all our spiritual exercises, the Rosary, spiritual readings, and all the other exercises that we have. Note carefully that they are the *means*, not the end of our spiritual and community life. They are the *means* by which we obtain the grace, and the enthusiasm, and the desire to do *what* God wants, *when* He wants it, which is often precisely when we feel least like doing it ourselves, when there is no satisfaction in it for ourselves. All of our spiritual exercises are the means whereby we obtain the grace to live as Mary did, to fit us and strengthen us to unite our wills with God's will, that is, to *do* what He *wants*, and to *want* what He *does*.

Our spiritual exercises are the implements which God has furnished us to get the grace to do everything that we know God wants us to do, particularly through *obedience* and *charity*. They are the means also by which we get the grace to want what God does, by *abandonment* of ourselves to all the circumstances of life which we might not like.

God has given us these means for our supernatural life, and our Blessed Lady, who is our perfect mother, is very interested in our *use* of these means. Each of them, when used properly, is a source of grace which comes from God the Holy Spirit, the Sanctifier; but it comes to us through the hands of Mary for she is the dispensatrix of all graces. So, she and the Holy Spirit are working hand in glove for our sanctification. Since, then, every grace given to us passes through her hands, she is very interested in our use of the means of grace and perfection, just as a natural mother is interested in her child's use of the means for bringing about his perfection.

A natural mother takes care of her child's physical needs by cooking, sewing, furnishing him shelter, and keeping the house for him; she takes care of his mental needs by seeing to it that he goes to school; by helping him with his studies;

by joining the P. T. A. so that she can integrate and cooperate with the school in her child's best interests. She sees that he *uses* all the means she can provide to develop into full adulthood. So, to, our Blessed Lady is interested in us, her children, and in our use of the means for achieving perfection in our spiritual life. She is ever ready to obtain grace for us and guide us to the union of our wills with God. But she is especially interested in the use we make of the means of grace to advance toward perfection which God has given us in our spiritual exercises.

Therefore, she is anxious to give us the help we need in order first of all, to be *faithful* in performing our spiritual exercises. Secondly, she is anxious to give us the grace to carry them out *as she would.* In other words, she is our model not only in our daily duty, but also in the performance of our spiritual exercises. She lived a life like ours; she did nothing that we do not do all day long; she combined prosaic worldly work with spiritual exercises. Therefore she wants us to call on her for the grace to be faithful to our spiritual exercises, and to perform them after her model.

Mary's Prayer Life and Ours

What do we read about spiritual exercises in Mary's life? Certainly, hers was a life of prayer. Saint Luke says: "But Mary kept in mind all these words, pondering them in her heart." She was so absorbed with communing with God that she was ever conscious of her union with Him. "My soul magnifies the Lord, and my spirit rejoices in God, my savior." So united was our Blessed Lady with God, that in each and every external event of her life, whether it was propitious or unfortunate, or disagreeable, or happy, she saw the divine plan. In each happening, in all the people with whom she came in contact, from the shepherds at the crib to the cruel soldiers of Herod chasing Him out of the city, she saw the divine plan, she saw God's message for her. Because she was united with God in prayer, she could see the supernatural beneath the natural in every contact with creatures.

As prayer was Mary's life, so, too, prayer is the warp and the woof of our life. As we pray our vocal prayers, what better way to be recollected than by having Mary kneeling in the pew beside us. Suppose our Blessed Lady were in the pew by our side today, as we were saying the Rosary, or as we say night prayers tonight. Imagine how we would be holding our beads, and how we would be looking out the corner of our eye to see the expression on her face, and to observe her interest in her prayers. How we would try to catch every nuance of her devotion! However, since this cannot be a physical reality, what a help it would be to keep our Blessed Lady kneeling beside us *in spirit* as we say our vocal prayers, our Rosary, our morning or night prayers.

The same method would give us untold help with our meditation or mental prayer, which occupies such an important segment of our lives. If we ponder God's message, if we keep all those words in our heart that we think of in meditation, keep them in our recollection during the course of the day, we, like Mary, shall see God and God's hand in all the events of our lives. We'll see all the things that happen to us as part of God's Providence and God's plan for us. Even the disagreeable things, and the hurtful things, we will see as Francis Thompson saw them, merely as the "shadow of His hand outstretched caressingly."

Mary and Our Spiritual Exercises

Again, what more fruitful way could we make our daily visit to the Blessed Sacrament than in the company of our Blessed Lady? Imagine, as we go to visit the Blessed Sacrament, that she were taking us into the back room of her little home in Nazareth and saying, "Sh! Don't wake him. He is sleeping." Look over the side of the crib at the Infant Jesus with her and say to Him in the tabernacle what we would say then. Or, let her take us to peek in through the back door of the carpenter shop as He works with Saint Joseph; or try to see Him through her eyes, or side by side with her as we catch a glimpse of Him when we turn a corner in the Holy City during His public life. If we would only take her with us on our visits to the Blessed Sacrament, how much more fruitful they would be. Ask her for the faith to see Him as truly in the Holy Eucharist as she saw Him on earth, and as she was able to see Him in the Blessed Sacrament at the Mass of Saint John after His Ascension. Ask her to obtain for us that Jesus in the Blessed Sacrament be our consolation as He was her consolation after He ascended into heaven.

Our examens can also be helped by making them in company with Mary. At that time, we should ask her for the grace we need to know our faults, the grace we need to see the mistakes we have made, and particularly, the grace we need to overcome our faults and to persevere in our resolutions. She is our mother, and we know how a mother would be interested in her child's struggle to be better—struggles to overcome some bad habit or habits. We know how she would sympathize and try to do everything she could to help her child improve. If any mother would do all that, how much more will not our mother Mary do?

As we listen to the readings each day, whether in the refectory or at the community reading in common, what a help it would be to think of the childhood of our Blessed Lady spent in the Temple after her presentation. We do not know for certain whether our Blessed Lady ever knew how to read or write, but we are told that she probably did not because Jewish girls at that time were not instructed in those arts. In spite of this, she was saturated with a knowledge of the

Scriptures, which she learned, most likely, from hearing them read in the Temple. The intensity with which she listened, the attention and the love with which she heard the words of God, so inculcated them in her mind that when she came to recite the Magnificat in the house of Elizabeth, that spontaneous prayer poured from her heart made up almost completely of verses and sections and phrases of the Old Testament. They were so close to the surface of her heart and her lips that they welled out in a fluster when she was moved by the Spirit to pray. From her, then, we can learn and ask for the grace to be attentive at reading, to be filled with a desire to listen to and hear the word of God in the way she did in the Temple.

Again, to make the Stations of the Cross in company with Mary will assure us of greater devotion in that incomparable exercise. Imagine the sentiments of Mary when that sorrowful journey was over. Imagine standing by her side as she looked into the tomb of her Son; it is not hard to put ourselves there. Surely we know how we would try to comfort her had we been there in reality. As at the end of the Stations, so it is possible to see every Station through the eyes of Mary, to make them in company with her. This wonderful opportunity is ours to live in union with Mary, our mother, to make her our wonderful companion at every waking moment of our lives. There is no need of anyone ever being lonely when Mary is with us.

Mary's Mass and Ours

The same method of union with Mary is available to us while participating in the greatest of all means for perfection which God has given us, the Holy Sacrifice of the Mass. The most perfect assistance in the Mass that we could have is to do it in conjunction with Mary. From her, we can learn to be not only good offerers of the sacrifice, but also good victims in being offered to God in the Mass.

As we know, the Mass is an action that we go to take part in. It is a public act of worship in which we offer to God His own Divine Son and ourselves as part of the Mystical Body of that same Divine Son. We offer Him all of our joys, and our sorrows, and our pain, and our anguish, and our happiness, and above all, we offer Him our wills.

In making this offering, Mary is the most perfect example we can have. No one ever so perfectly united herself with Christ during the sacrifice of Calvary. Nobody ever so perfectly offered *Christ* to God; nobody ever offered *herself* so perfectly in union with Christ. Mary at the foot of the cross is our model for participation in the Mass. She demonstrated an absolute, complete conformity of her will to the will of the Father. In the midst of this awful tragedy, holding the broken, dead body of her own precious Son in her arms, she still had the faith to believe the cry of the Father, "This is my beloved Son, in whom I am well pleased." God loved Him, and therefore, even though she could not understand how this was a manifestation of love, it must be because God said so. Therefore, she said, "Fiat!" to it. "Fiat!" Her will was united to that of her Son and to that of the Father, which was the same will.

This fiat of hers was not merely some kind of helpless, passive surrender; it was not mere mute, numb, endurance of this awful offering, of this awful tragedy. No mother can be passive at the death of her own son. She gave freely, and she gave generously what was nearest and dearest to her, her own Son. Along with Him, she gave herself. So completely did she give herself in the midst of that awful sacrifice, during that awful tragedy of Calvary, that because of it she merited to be called the Queen of Martyrs and the Co-redemptrix of the human race.

Can we imagine the sentiments with which our Blessed

Lady assisted at Mass at the house of Saint John where she lived after the Resurrection and Ascension of her Son? He had given her into the keeping of Saint John; Saint John, of course, priest and bishop as he was, offered the holy sacrifice of the Mass. Who of us can fathom how our Blessed Lady united her will completely in that offering, knowing that this was the same death of her Son she had so recently witnessed on Calvary, being re-presented to the Father. Imagine what her sentiments must have been. Can we imagine her being distracted at Mass? Can we picture her being bored at Mass?

After the death of her Son and His Resurrection, she continued to offer herself in the Mass in the same way she did on Calvary. She continued to offer herself up to God, to offer her will to Him again in the Mass. She let the Body and Blood of her Son consecrated separately on the altar be a sign to God, not only of the sacrifice of her Son, but also of the immolation of her own will; a sign that she was disposed to let His grace work in her; a sign that her will was united to His, let Him ask what He would; a sign that she was willing to spend herself for the spread of His kingdom.

So, when we kneel at Mass, how could we better take part in that sacrifice than to imagine Mary kneeling beside us, and try to participate in the Mass in the same dispositions that she would have; to reproduce in ourselves the dispositions that we know we would have, weak as we are, if she were physically there beside us.

Mary and Our Holy Communion

Furthermore, just as we should think of Mary and ask her help, and have her with us when we assist in the *sacrifice* of the Mass, so we should do likewise when we participate in the *sacramental* element of the Mass, that is, when we receive Holy Communion. Holy Communion is a channel of grace. It is a source of an avalanche of graces that comes into our hearts each time we receive it. But we must not forget that the graces of Holy Communion come to us in the same way the graces of any sacrament come, namely, from Christ through the immaculate and precious hands of our Lady herself. Not only does she dispense what she receives from Him, not only does she pass them on to us, but she had a tremendous share in the very earning of them, because she was the co-redeemer of the human race.

Therefore, at thanksgiving, what greater help to be grateful can we have than that of Mary the mother of grace. At Bethlehem, the poverty, and the coldness, and the dirt and the squalor of the stable were all more than made up for by the love and the warmth of Mary's heart. The infant God in the manger of that stable was unconcerned about the cold, and the dirt, and the poverty, and the squalor. All He felt was the warmth and the love of Mary's heart.

So often, when we receive our Lord, our hearts are nothing but a stable. We are cold, we are distracted, we are sinful, we are bitter, we are unkind or unforgiving. In a word, we are sinners; we are everything that we know deep down in our hearts we are. But Mary can make up for all of that. She can fill our hearts with the warmth and fire of her love and her charity for Him. At communion, we should ask her to be in our hearts to help us to welcome Him. Ask her to sweep up the dirt and the dust in our heart, to clean it up, to make it look a little presentable for Him to come into this morning. When He comes, ask her to welcome Him for us, to make it warm and comfortable in our hearts for Him by her warmth; ask her to adore Him, her own Son; ask her for her help, the help we need for ourselves—the graces to overcome our temptations and our predominant fault; ask her for the help we need to carry on our duty; ask her for the graces we want for others, our loved ones, and those for whom we pray; ask her, above all, for the grace of final perseverance; ask her for the graces that she knows we need better than we know ourselves. What more profitable way to make thanksgiving after communion than to make it with Mary, and through Mary?

In our thanksgiving to our Lord, we will say a word ourselves. Above all, in thanking Him, let us never forget to thank Him for having given her to us as our mother. Let us thank Him for the opportunity which is ours to have her with us every hour of the day, every minute of every hour, Mary, our mother.

Importance of Avoiding Discouragement

Finally, we come to an end of our discussion of some basic spiritual means for living a healthy spiritual life and community life, means for being a Religious after the heart of our Lord Himself. But let no one be in the least discouraged at what may seem a discouraging task in his life. Our goal has been presented very clearly. But we are not at the goal; perhaps we are not expected to be at the goal. But if the goal were never pointed out to us, we would never begin to strive for it. For that reason, the objective has been delineated, and motives and means have been urged for striving toward it.

But, be it repeated, let no one be discouraged in that striving, for if we are discouraged, it is because we are trusting in ourselves and not in God. As a warning to those who trust in themselves, He has said, "Without me you can do nothing." But to those who trust in Him, He has given the words of Saint Paul, "I can do all things in him who strengthens me."

Our determination, our conviction, then, should be to trust in God; to recognize that all He wants is our puny efforts; that all He wants is for us to say, "Dear God, I will *try;* but I know You will be behind me, doing the work. I won't be the one that is doing it." What He wants is for us to try, just to try. Above all, He wants us to tell Him with all our hearts we at least *want* to try. He wants us even to *pray* to be able to say, "Dear God, I want to try." He will be satisfied with that for a beginning. And if we pray to Mary, she can not help obtaining that grace for us, the grace to say to her Son with all our heart, "Dear God, you know I want to try."